CULTURES OF THE WORLD

GHANA

Patricia Levy

MARSHALL CAVENDISH
New York • London • Sydney

Reference edition reprinted 2002 by
Marshall Cavendish Corporation
99 White Plains Road
Tarrytown, NY 10591
Website: www.marshallcavendish.com

© Times Media Private Limited 1999
First published 1999
Reprinted 2000, 2002

Originated and designed by
Times Books International, an imprint of
Times Media Private Limited, a member of the
Times Publishing Group

Printed in Malaysia

Library of Congress Cataloging-in-Publication Data:
Levy, Patricia, 1951–.
    Ghana / Patricia Levy.
        p. cm. — (Cultures of the World)
    Includes bibliographical references and index.
    Summary: Describes the geography, history, government,
economy, people, lifestyle, religion, language, arts, leisure,
festivals, and food of Ghana.
    ISBN 0-7614-0952-1 (library binding)
    1. Ghana—Juvenile literature. [1. Ghana.] I. Title.
II. Series.
    DT510.L48   1999
    966.7—dc21   98-49004
                            CIP
                            AC

INTRODUCTION

THE WEST AFRICAN REPUBLIC OF GHANA takes its name from the ancient kingdom of Ghana that once flourished far to the north of the modern state. First a loose union of warring tribes and later a British colony named the Gold Coast, Ghana has been an independent state since 1957.

One of the more prosperous African states, Ghana has seen little of the wars and strife that have plagued many of its neighbors in recent years. Its culture is a combination of African tradition and British influence, and its people are proud of their forward-looking modern state. With its vast untapped natural resources and peaceful political scene, Ghana is set to become a leading member of the African and world community in the 21st century. This book in the *Cultures of the World* series celebrates its land, lifestyles, culture, and peoples.

CONTENTS

A bamboo and rattan shop displays its wares.

CONTENTS

A Ghanaian boy.

GEOGRAPHY

GHANA IS LOCATED IN WEST AFRICA, 400 miles (644 km) north of the equator, in the Gulf of Guinea, which forms 335 miles (539 km) of its southern border. To the north lies Burkina Faso, to the west is Côte d'Ivoire, and to the east is Togo. With a total land area of 92,100 square miles (238,539 sq km), Ghana is about the same size as Great Britain.

About 4.5 billion years ago Ghana was part of a supercontinent called Gondwanaland, made up of present-day South America, Africa, India, and Australia. Some 600 million years ago the land sank, creating a huge interior lake within Ghana. The Mesozoic era, 220 million years ago, saw the breakup of the supercontinent and the creation of the separate continent of Africa. Later still, around 70 million years ago, the land was forced upward, forming the modern topography of Ghana. Ghana consists of four regions—the coastal plain, the forest-dissected plateau, the savanna high plains, and the Voltaian sandstone basin.

Ancient metamorphic rock formations that date back to when Ghana was part of Gondwanaland can still be seen in the Accra Plains and the southern part of the Volta region.

Opposite: **A hilly road in eastern Ghana, near the Togo border.**

Left: **The southwestern coast of Ghana.**

To the east, Ghana's coastline is made up of the Volta Delta and a series of sandbars, while to the west the land is hilly and consists of bays and headlands. The eastern coast contains many marshes, lagoons, and mangrove swamps.

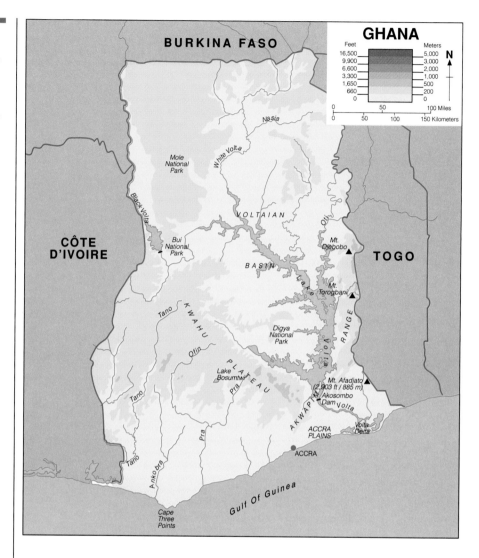

TOPOGRAPHY

THE COASTAL PLAIN This long strip of land, which includes most of the coastline of Ghana, stretches 50 miles (80 km) inland at its eastern and western ends, but narrows to around 10 miles (16 km) in the middle. Divided in half by the capital city of Accra, the coastal plain is low-lying, with an average elevation of 246 feet (75 m) above sea level. Some areas, such as the lagoon at Kéta, are below sea level and occasionally flood.

THE FOREST-DISSECTED PLATEAU The plateau occupies a large triangular area of the southwest of Ghana, including part of the southern coast. The landscape is mostly gently rolling hills, with broad, flat valleys between. The region consists of primary rainforest in the extreme southwest, with plantations of hardwood and cocoa trees making up the rest of the plateau.

THE SAVANNA HIGH PLAINS This inverted L-shaped band of land in the north and northwest of the country averages 600–1,000 feet (180–300 m) above sea level and is made up of gently undulating plains with occasional small, rounded hills.

The land is dry and covered in tall grasses, some reaching 12 feet (3.7 m), low bushes, and the occasional tree. Because of the underlying rock, some parts are swampy. From November to March there is no rain in this region and the land dries out completely. Nevertheless, the plants survive as they have adapted to withstand long periods of drought.

Savanna-like vegetation dominates the landscape in the north.

THE VOLTAIAN SANDSTONE BASIN This consists of around 43,540 square miles (112,770 sq km) of land in the eastern half of the country. Like the northwest, it is covered in savanna-like vegetation, but is lower-lying and flatter, at around 200 to 600 feet (60 to 180 m) above sea level. Around its edges are several ridges and mountains.

To the east is the Akwapim range, which includes Mount Afadjato, Ghana's highest point, while to the west is a long narrow plateau. At its heart is the water system of Lake Volta.

The northeastern part of Ghana is considerably drier than the southwestern region.

CLIMATE

Although close to the equator, Ghana has a moderate climate with sunshine throughout the year and constant, cooling breezes. The southwest is hot and humid, while the east is dry. In the north temperatures during the dry season can reach 100°F (38°C). Nowhere in Ghana do average temperatures fall below 77°F (25°C). The hottest time of the year in the south is usually April, just before the long wet season. The coldest is August, just after the wet season. All of Ghana experiences the dry and wet seasons, but the effect of the dry season is less noticeable in the south. The coastal area and the forested areas have two wet seasons—a long season between April and July and a shorter rainy season from September to November. The north experiences only one wet season between September and November.

RAINFALL

Ghana is affected by two large air masses—one flows northward from the south Atlantic, while the other flows south from the Sahara. The first is a humid, warm body of air that keeps day and night temperatures at around 77°F (25°C). The second is very dry and brings hot daytime temperatures, low nighttime temperatures, and clear skies.

These two air masses effectively create regional weather conditions in Ghana. The extreme southwest of the country is the most influenced by the southern air mass. It receives about 75 inches (190 cm) of rain a year. As the air mass moves north, it loses water, so the northern part of the country receives much less rain. The southeast of the country sees the lowest rainfall of around 29 inches (74 cm) a year. Here the land is flat so the clouds move by without releasing any water.

The coastal region near Cape Coast. The air mass from the south influences Ghana's weather so that it is often cloudy. The air mass only sheds its water when forced to rise over mountains.

THE HARMATTAN

The harmattan is a wind that affects large areas of Africa. It originates in the Sahara and blows across Ghana from the north and northeast. It is a hot, dry wind and carries a large amount of red dust, which is deposited throughout the country. The forested areas in the southwest of the country break up this wind and protect the southwest from its drying influence.

The harmattan can be devastating. In 1983 it blew across the entire country, disrupting the rainy season and causing a major drought that resulted in serious food shortages. Famine was only avoided by the arrival of food donated by other countries.

WATER SYSTEMS

Ghana's river systems are fed by both rainfall and mountain springs. In the north of the country some rivers that only receive rainwater are either flooded during the rainy season or are completely dry in the dry season. Water volume in spring-fed streams declines in the dry season, but the streams do not dry up completely. In the forested zone, where rainfall is more consistent, the rivers flow throughout the year. In the west of Ghana several small rivers flow into the Gulf of Guinea; the Pra, the Ankobra, and the Tano are the largest. These are permanent rivers, but are barely navigable as they have many rapids and waterfalls.

Fishermen on Lake Volta's northern shore.

THE DAMMING OF THE VOLTA RIVER

Construction of a dam on the Volta River began in 1961, and the dam was in operation by 1966. A lake was created that stretches 250 miles (402 km) behind the dam. The lake flooded 2.1 million acres (850,500 hectares) of inhabited land (one-seventh of Ghana's total landmass) and 80,000 people had to be resettled. The hydroelectric power generated by the dam supplies a power grid covering southern Ghana and extending into Togo.

The lake provides an inland transportation system that reduces the cost of transporting goods from the north to the south of the country. Its waters irrigate parts of the Accra Plains, which has no steady source of water, and it has added huge numbers of fish to the country's fishing stocks. It is likely too, in the long term, to affect the country's climate by making the area more humid and by increasing rainfall.

Lake Volta is the world's largest artificial lake. Its dam stands 407 feet (124 m) high.

Ghana has only one natural lake, Bosumtwi in the south central interior. About 19 square miles (49 sq km) in area, the lake is almost perfectly round and may have been created by volcanic activity. It is surrounded by high hills. Streams in the hills feed the lake, many of them flowing around the lake before entering it.

There are several lagoons, the largest of which is the lagoon at Kéta in the southeast.

THE VOLTA RIVER Ghana's longest river is fed by three major tributaries. The Black Volta rises in Burkina Faso, where it is called the Baoule, travels along Ghana's border with Côte d'Ivoire, and flows into the Volta. The White Volta also rises in Burkina Faso, but flows almost due south to join the Volta. Both these rivers are not navigable during the dry season, but flood during the wet season. A third river, the Oti, also feeds the Volta River. The Oti rises in Burkina Faso, crosses Togo, and enters Ghana to join the Volta.

In 1966 the Volta was dammed at Akosombo to create a hydroelectric power station. A second dam has been created farther south, while the Black Volta has been dammed at Bui in the northwest of the country.

Rainforest in Ghana. The forest has three layers. Tall trees of 115–150 feet (35–45 m) form the canopy. These trees have wide crowns and buttresses at their roots to stabilize them in the shallow soil. A second group of trees with narrower crowns grow to a height of 50–80 feet (15–25 m). Below this is the underbrush consisting of young trees and plants that have adapted to survive in the deep shade of the forest floor. The underbrush is sparse so walking through the rainforest is relatively easy. Lianas and other climbing plants trail up the trees to reach sunlight.

FLORA AND FAUNA

Ghana has several different zones, determined by rainfall and human activity. In the southwest is the tropical rainforest. Farther east and north is a large band of deciduous forest. Here the taller trees lose their leaves in the dry season. However, the lower layers of trees do not lose their leaves and benefit from the leafless season of the higher trees. In Ghana most of this area is secondary forest—forest land that was once logged and cultivated but has since been reclaimed by the forest.

The forest gradually gives way to the grasses and bushes of the savanna. This region, midway between deciduous forest and savanna, is the largest vegetation zone in Ghana, covering about 65,600 square miles (170,000 sq km). Trees found in this region include the baobab, acacia, and the shea tree. In the wet season such vegetation becomes very green. Tall grasses, up to 10 feet (3 m) high, cover the ground, waving gently in the breeze. In the dry season the trees lose their leaves and the grasses turn yellow.

An interesting sight in the dry savanna areas of Ghana are the huge termite mounds that look like miniature mud palaces. The termites live underground and the tall towers of the mound are designed to bring air into the nest.

THE BAOBAB TREE

This is an unusual tree that the people of Ghana use in many ways. It grows throughout Africa in savanna areas and looks as if it has been turned upside down, with the branches buried in the soil and the roots sticking up in the air. It can grow to a girth of 30 feet (9 m) and as high as 60 feet (18 m).

The fruit of the tree is large and gourdlike and can be eaten. The trunk is often hewn and hollowed out to make barrels used to collect and store rain water. The bark can be made into rope and cloth, while the tree itself provides shade in many villages and is often the site of the village school.

In the southeast of the country is an area of coastal grassland. This area receives little rain but is very humid. The few trees here include the baobab and nim, while in the wetter areas wild oil palms and fan palms grow.

Around the coastal lagoons and the Volta River in the southeast are mangrove swamps where the vegetation has adapted to living in salt water. Mangrove trees grow to about 50 feet (15 m) and have tall aerial roots that help the plant keep stable in the soft mud of tidal waters.

Ghana has a rich and diverse animal life, although like the forests this is under serious threat because of the steadily increasing human population. Ghana has over 200 species of mammals, including elephants, leopards, wild buffalo, antelope, many kinds of primates, hyenas, and wild pigs. Crocodiles and hippos are common along the rivers, and many species of poisonous snakes pose a danger to people. Cobras, puff adders, and horned adders can kill with their venomous bite, while pythons can squeeze their victims to death. About 300 species of birds live in Ghana, from huge eagles to tiny swallows.

*Opposite:***Accra has been the capital of the Gold Coast since 1877, and of Ghana since independence.**

EROSION

Like many other countries where the population is growing, the land in Ghana is coming under increasing pressure as villages expand and the soil becomes depleted. Improved irrigation in the Voltaian Basin has encouraged people to raise cattle, and large areas of the savanna are being denuded due to overgrazing.

The forested areas are being logged and turned into grassland, which in turn becomes infertile and overgrazed. The result is erosion, as torrential rains fall on what was once vegetation but is now bare soil. Much of the rainforest that has been logged has not been replanted. The government has created protected reserves where trees cannot be logged and where animals are safe from hunters. Similar solutions will have to be found for the grasslands and cultivated land around the major cities, where the land is not left fallow long enough for the vegetation to reestablish itself.

MAJOR CITIES

ACCRA The capital city of Ghana, Accra, has a population of 1,200,000 (1994). Located on the coastal plain, it is an old city that was first settled in 1482 when the Portuguese arrived in Ghana. Colonized in turn by the Dutch, English, and Danes in the 17th century, it grew into a prosperous trading center.

Accra is the administrative and financial center of Ghana and has a hospital, a medical school, three cathedrals, and a museum. The University of Ghana was founded in 1948. A soccer stadium and race course provide for leisure activities, while the Black Star Square is the center of cultural activities. Accra has an international airport and bus and rail links to other towns.

Its main industries are food processing and the manufacture of textiles and lumber. Most of Ghana's imports arrive at Tema, 27 miles (43 km) to the east of the city center, and are then transported to Accra to be distributed around the country.

Like many cities in Africa, Accra has a mix of rich and poor. The relatively well-off own houses, cars, and electrical goods, while others live in shantytowns with poor sanitation and own few possessions.

Set on hills and surrounded by forest, Kumasi has a humid climate with high rainfall and is known as a garden city.

KUMASI   This is Ghana's second largest town, with a population of 800,000 (1994). Kumasi is located in south-central Ghana, about 200 miles (322 km) northwest of Accra. It, too, is an ancient city and was the 17th century capital of the Ashanti kingdom. Kumasi is situated at the junction of main roads and is the main transit point for goods coming from the interior to Accra and the seaports. It has teacher-training colleges, the University of Science and Technology, and agricultural research institutions.

The area around Kumasi is dedicated to cocoa farming, which brings in much of the city's wealth. The Ashanti people, who still keep their capital at Kumasi, make the famous *kente* ("KEN-tey") cloth, which is a profitable cottage industry. Kumasi has an armed forces museum in an old British fort and a cultural center. Kumasi also has the largest market in Ghana, selling everything from crafts to auto parts.

OTHER TOWNS The major town in the north of Ghana is Tamale, with a population of 220,000. It was developed as a town around 1907 when the British chose it as the administrative center of the northern region, a position it still holds. Other large towns in the north include Yendi and Bolgatanga, both built along the main roads of the north. Bolgatanga is the most northerly major town and has a population of about 50,000 (1994). It serves as an administrative center for the Frafra district.

Along the coast are a series of towns first established by European colonists, such as Sekondi-Takoradi, Cape Coast, Elmina, and Saltpond, with populations of 300,000 or less. Sekondi-Takoradi is a port city and has an artificial harbor. It also has sawmills, paper factories, and an airport for light aircraft. Cape Coast is known as an educational center and has many schools, colleges, and a university.

Tamale acts as a distribution and collection center for the produce of the northern region. Cotton, rice, butter, and peanuts are collected here and shipped to Accra. Tamale has a small airstrip and there are plans for a larger airport. It also has a fruit-canning factory.

HISTORY

THE COUNTRY KNOWN TODAY as Ghana has had that name only since independence in 1957. It took the name from an ancient kingdom far to the north of modern Ghana, and while many Ghanaians believe they are the descendants of that early empire, most historians believe otherwise. Before independence Ghana was known as the Gold Coast.

EARLY HISTORY

Little is known about the early inhabitants of Ghana. Stone tools dating back to 5500–2500 B.C. found in the plains around Accra suggest a hunter-gatherer community of people who lived by the sea and moved around, gathering berries and wild seeds and hunting animals. The oral traditions of some of the tribes in Ghana also reveal a little about their early history. For example, stories by the Ewe people, who live in the southeast of

Opposite: **Black Star Square in Accra has been the site of many public ceremonies since Ghana's independence in 1957.**

Left: **Ghanaians celebrate their Independence Day with a parade.**

Elmina Castle, a legacy of the early Portuguese traders.

Ghana, say that they emigrated to Ghana around A.D. 1600 after being driven out of modern Benin by another tribe. The Ga and Adangme, who live in the area around Accra, believe their ancestors came from southern Nigeria during the 16th century and conquered another tribe of people called the Guan. The Ga founded a small state called the kingdom of Accra, whose capital was inland from the modern city.

The oral tradition of the inland Akan people say that they first lived in Ghana around the 13th century in the northwest grasslands. As the Akan kingdom grew, groups migrated south to the forested areas and farther south to the coast.

ANCIENT TRADE ROUTES

Long before the arrival of the Europeans to the west coast of Africa, these kingdoms traded with one another and with tribes from farther afield. The northwest trade route ran south from the ancient kingdom of Mali through modern Ghana and then south to modern Nigeria. From the central trading town of Kumasi in central Ghana more trade routes went to the coast. Along the trade routes from the north came caravans carrying dates, salt, tobacco, and copper. The settlements of Ghana traded cloth, ostrich feathers, and tanned hides as well as cola nuts and slaves.

After 1591 great changes took place in Ghana's trading patterns and in the future course of its history. That year war broke out between the Songhai empire, Ghana's chief trading partner to the north, and the Moors of North Africa. As a result, the Songhai empire fell into decline, and the trade with the north ended.

ARRIVAL OF THE EUROPEANS

More than a century earlier, in 1471, Portuguese traders had arrived near Elmina on the southwest coast. Their original intention was to find a sea route to the lucrative markets of the Far East, and they sailed along the coast of Africa searching for this route. Venturing ashore, they discovered that the local people wore gold jewelry. The traders reported this to King John II. In 1481 a special mission led by Diogo d'Azambuja was sent to Ghana. It discovered much gold and in 1482 built a fort at Elmina. Trade between Portugal and the tribes of Ghana flourished, with gold dominating trade. The Portuguese later built more forts—at Axim, Shama, and Accra—to store the gold while their trading ships were at sea and to protect the Portuguese from both the indigenous people and the English and Dutch, who were also exploring the area.

King John II of Portugal encouraged exploration of new lands and fostered trade with Africa.

In 1598 the Dutch began building forts at Mouri, Butri, Kormantsi, and Komeda, all along the southern coast of Ghana. There was fierce competition between the Dutch and Portuguese for control of the area, and in 1637 and 1642 the Dutch captured two Portuguese forts. During the 17th century the English, Germans, and Danes also built forts. Eager for ivory and gold, they brought rum, cotton, cloth, beads, mirrors, and guns and gunpowder to exchange with the local people.

The European traders competed with one another for favor with the local tribes. They paid rent for their forts to the local chiefs and respected the chiefs' rule that they not venture into the interior but remain in the coastal forts where goods were brought to them. Occasionally the Europeans were expected to give their help in intertribal battles.

THE ASHANTI

When the Akan people first migrated into Ghana some settled around the confluence of the Pra and Ofin rivers. As the kingdom grew, some families moved north and founded the powerful Ashanti empire in the Kumasi area.

During the 17th century a tribal chief called Osei Tutu formed an alliance of the various tribes in the area. He built the capital town of Kumasi and established a golden stool as a symbol of his power. He created a national army and expanded his empire, which he ruled well. Osei Tutu also astutely offered tribal leaders he conquered important jobs in his kingdom. Other chiefs under his rule agreed to pay taxes for the purchase of guns and to travel to the capital whenever they were summoned.

In 1698 the Ashanti began a war with a neighboring kingdom, the Denkyera. This kingdom stood between the Ashanti and the coast and controlled all their trade. After three years, the Denkyera were defeated. Under the next king of the Ashanti, Opuku Ware, more tribes in the interior were conquered until by 1750, most of the tribes of the interior formed part of the Ashanti empire. The last kingdom to hold out against the power of the Ashanti was the Fanti empire, which dominated the coastal area, and with it the trade with the Europeans. In 1750 Opuku Ware died and civil war broke out between his potential successors. Several subject kingdoms seized the opportunity to declare their independence and joined the Fanti empire. After this the Ashanti empire began to decline, weakened by wars and a series of bad kings.

Osei Bosu became ruler of the Ashanti in 1801, and under his rule the strength of the Ashanti grew once more. His armies finally defeated the Fanti in 1807, and the Ashanti became the most powerful empire in West Africa, controlling most of modern Ghana.

Osei Kwame (1777–1801) was a particularly bad king. He murdered many of his family members and sacrificed ordinary people at the funerals of his relatives.

THE SLAVE TRADE

When the Europeans first began to trade with the people of Ghana their chief interests were gold and ivory, but another commodity quickly became even more profitable. In the West Indies and in the southern colonies of the Americas huge sugar and cotton plantations needed a source of cheap labor. The Europeans supplied the tribes with guns that made possible the tribal wars between the Ashanti and its neighbors. Countless slaves were taken in battle.

By the early 1700s slavery was the most important trade between the Europeans and the African tribes. Ashanti raiding parties penetrated the interior and captured people whom they brought to the coastal forts to sell. The forts became prisons, holding pens, and slave markets. Hundreds of people were thrown into the holds of trading ships for the journey to the Americas. Many died from disease or starvation, or were murdered by the ships' captains.

The slave trade continued for another hundred years, making the Ashanti the richest and most powerful empire in West Africa. The trade was finally stopped early in the 19th century, when first Denmark, then Britain outlawed the slave trade and sent ships to attack the slave ships and return them to Africa.

THE BRITISH IN GHANA

By the time the Europeans settled on the coast of Ghana, the British had developed trading relations with the Fanti tribe. They saw the growing power of the Ashanti as a threat to their own power. The Ashanti began attacking British forts, while the British provided military support to the Fanti. When the slave trade was abolished in Europe, the British hoped that by destroying the Ashanti they could end the slave trade in Africa.

In 1821 a British governor was sent to administer the area, but he was killed by the Ashanti in 1824. The British eventually defeated the Ashanti in 1826. In 1829 George Maclean was sent to Ghana to sign a peace treaty

The British in a conference with Ashanti tribal chiefs in the 1870s.

with the Ashanti. The British agreed to protect Ashanti traders and to arbitrate in intertribal quarrels. On their part, the Ashanti and other tribes agreed to stop human sacrifices, and to keep the peace. In this new peace trade again began to flourish. Palm oil, pepper, and corn were added to gold and ivory as important exports, while imports included tools, alcohol, tobacco, and guns.

In 1844 the British sent out a new governor to work with Maclean. The governor and his successors began to raise taxes among the local tribes to finance road building. This was very unpopular and led to attacks on British trading posts. In 1867 the British and Dutch agreed to divide the Ghanaian coast between them, with the British taking the east and the Dutch the west.

In 1868 the Fanti organized a confederation to oppose the British and defend themselves against the Ashanti. The British saw this confederation as a threat to their authority and arrested its rulers, leaving the confederation to fade away. The British began buying all the Dutch forts and by 1874 became the sole European power in Ghana.

With the Fanti confederacy weakened, the main remaining threat was the Ashanti, who lost their allies and source of guns when the Dutch left. The British attacked the Ashanti in 1874, burning their capital, Kumasi. Initially they allowed the Ashanti independence, but in 1891, fearing that the French might annex the Ashanti territories, they declared Ashanti a protectorate. The Ashanti challenged the declaration. In 1896 the British attacked Kumasi a second time, exiling the ruler to Sierra Leone. In the 1890s the British extended their power to the north of Ghana, and by 1902, the borders formed the British colony called the Gold Coast.

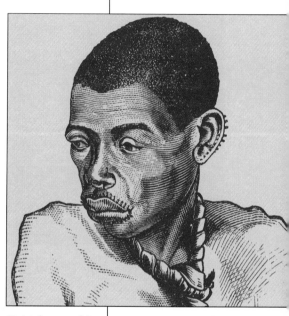

A drawing of a slave offered in the market. The Ashanti amassed their wealth and power from supplying slaves to Europeans until the early 19th century.

The University of Ghana at Legon, near Accra, was established in 1948 by the British.

THE 20TH CENTURY: A BRITISH COLONY

Ghana had reluctantly become a colony in the British empire. In the past the British had maintained only enough control to keep the exports flowing, but once Ghana was a colony the priorities changed. A governor was appointed, with two councils (the legislative and executive councils), to help him make decisions. All the people who sat on these councils were British until 1914, when nine of the legislative councillors were Ghanaians. In 1943 two Africans joined the executive council. The legislative council functioned as a ratifying body for the laws that the governor introduced. Using a system of indirect rule, where the local chiefs acted as executives of the governor's laws, the British bypassed the intellectual elite of Ghana who might have challenged British authority if they were given any power.

Nevertheless, the British brought peace and development to Ghana. The first gold mines were developed, where previously gold dust had been panned from rivers. Manganese, bauxite, and diamond mines were also developed. Railways were built to carry the products of the mines to the coast, and harbors were constructed for the ships that came to collect the exports. The government distributed cocoa beans to local farmers and encouraged the cocoa industry. Towns grew as a result of trade and the railways. The government also built hospitals.

For many Ghanaians, however, these gestures were inadequate compensation for the massive profits that British companies were making from the labor of the Ghanaians. Until 1948 there were no universities in Ghana; if an African wanted a university education he had to go overseas to study.

GROWING NATIONALISM

One of the students who went abroad was Kwame Nkrumah. In the United States, he studied Marx and the writings of African Americans and developed radical ideas about independence for Ghana. In Ghana at this time there was a pro-independence party that campaigned for a gradual shift to independence.

In 1947 Nkrumah broke away from this party and with the slogan "self-government now" formed a more vocal and radical party, the Convention People's Party (CPP). In 1951, when Nkrumah was in jail, the CPP won the general election. Nkrumah was released and asked to form a government. For six years Nkrumah and his party compromised, working with the colonial powers and at the same time learning about government. In 1957 power passed peacefully to the people of Ghana when Britain granted the country independence.

A charismatic leader, Kwame Nkrumah led Ghana to independence in 1957.

INDEPENDENCE AND BEYOND

Ghana was the first African colony to gain political power; unfortunately it went into a tailspin. At independence Ghana held half a billion US dollars in reserves. Ten years later it was a billion dollars in debt. Foreign loans were taken out to finance ill-conceived projects such as the Akosombo Dam. Income plunged when the international price of cocoa collapsed. Many industries were nationalized and began to lose money. From a peak of popularity throughout Africa in 1957, Nkrumah gradually resorted to one-party rule and numerous arrests of political opponents to keep power. A coup attempt failed in 1962, but in 1966, while he was abroad, another coup was successfully carried out. Nkrumah never returned to Ghana.

A headless statue of Nkrumah lies toppled in the aftermath of the coup against him in 1966.

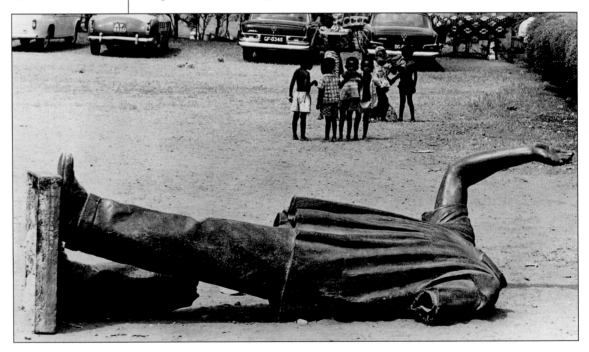

Between 1966 and 1981 a series of corrupt governments ran Ghana. For three years the government was run by a National Liberation Council and right-wing elements that hunted down left-wing politicians and parties. Nationalized industries were reprivatized. In 1969 elections were held and a politically moderate party took power. But the economy was so weak that food shortages and huge price increases developed. In 1972 another coup threw out this government. Military juntas took power, food prices stayed high, corruption became widespread, and political opponents were arrested.

In June 1979 yet another coup was led by Flight Lieutenant Jerry Rawlings. This takeover was, however, different from the earlier coups. Rawlings made the eradication of corruption his main promise and kept his word. Many corrupt officials were arrested and executed and within a few months Rawlings had given up power and established a new democratically elected government. But this government fared little better than the previous ones. A new set of corrupt politicians began siphoning off much needed state income.

In 1981 Rawlings led a second coup, promising again to remove corrupt practices and restore stability to the economy. This time, Rawlings decided to keep power and sort out the problems himself. Rawlings' ideas were very left-wing. There were several attempts by other factions of the army to depose him, but all failed. Rawlings remains popular with Ghanaians at the grassroots level and has overseen a gradual improvement in the economy. In 1996 Rawlings held general elections and was reelected to office. The economy has continued to grow and Rawlings is a popular figure in a stable country.

Ghanaians celebrate the inauguration of a new but ultimately short-lived government in 1969.

GOVERNMENT

SINCE 1981 THE GOVERNMENT has been led by Flight Lieutenant Jerry Rawlings, holding one position or another. He took power in a military coup, disbanded parliament, and banned political parties. The government was run by a Provisional National Defense Council, with Rawlings as chairman. A period of political stability followed, leading to a new constitution in 1992 that allows for a multiparty system. Besides the national government, there is a system of tribal governments led by chiefs.

THE CONSTITUTION

Four constitutions have been adopted since Ghana's independence. The current one describes a multiparty system, with one legislative house of 200 members elected by direct, universal adult suffrage. The executive element of the government is carried out by the president with a council

Opposite: **Cadets at a passing-out ceremony at Ghana's military academy.**

Left: **Elementary schoolchildren with the Ghanaian flag. Its colors are the pan-African red, yellow, and green. Red stands for revolution and the blood of those who fought for independence; yellow for the natural resources of the country, especially gold, and green for the green life of the country. The five-pointed star in the center of the yellow band represents African freedom.**

Government buildings in Accra.

of ministers approved by the legislature and a vice president. There is also a National Security Council, made up of senior ministers and members of the security forces.

THE PRESIDENT

The president is the head-of-state of Ghana and commander-in-chief of the armed forces. Jerry Rawlings, elected in 1992, was the first president to be elected under the present, fourth constitution. The president is elected by universal adult suffrage for a term of four years, with a possibility of a second term. In the 1992 election there were five candidates, with Rawlings taking 58% of the vote. A total of 48.3% of the electorate voted. As president, Rawlings is popular with the poorer citizens. He professes a left-leaning, Marxist ideology, while at the same time allowing a free-market policy that gives Ghana the healthiest and most prosperous economy in Africa.

THE MINISTRIES

The Council of Ministers is made up of the heads of the various departments of state: the ministers of defense, state, finance, parliamentary affairs, foreign affairs, justice, local government, education, the interior, food and agriculture, health, roads and transport, tourism, trade and industry, youth and sports, land and forestry, works and housing, communications, employment and social welfare, environment, science and technology, and mines and energy.

JERRY RAWLINGS

Jerry John Rawlings was born in 1947 to a Scottish father and Ghanaian mother. He was educated in Ghana, first at Achimoto College and then at the military college. In 1969 he was commissioned a lieutenant in the air force. Ten years later he led a military coup against the corrupt civilian government of General Ignatius Kutu. Kutu and many others were tried and executed. Rawlings kept power for 112 days and then called a general election. Two years later, after the failure of the next president to prevent corruption or improve the economy, Rawlings led a second coup and this time kept power, ruling with the aid of a Provisional National Defense Council.

Local committees were set up to monitor the work of factories and run local neighborhoods. In 1983 Rawlings switched from his Marxist policies to free-market ones, denationalizing state-owned industries, devaluing the currency, and abandoning price controls. All these measures were very unpopular, but people realized that he had Ghana's interests at heart and accepted them. Ghana has since become one of the few African countries with a healthy economy and relatively stable government.

In the 1996 presidential and parliamentary elections, Rawlings was reelected with 57% of the vote and his party, the National Democratic Congress, took 133 of the 200 seats in parliament.

A political poster for an opposition party.

POLITICAL PARTIES

During the first decade of Rawlings' rule, political parties were banned in Ghana. They were legalized for the 1992 election, although none of Ghana's previous parties were allowed to register for the election. The dominant political party in Ghana is the National Democratic Congress, led by Rawlings, with a few smaller parties such as the National Convention Party and some independents forming the opposition.

LOCAL GOVERNMENT

Democratically elected local governments were in place in Ghana in 1989. At the time, political parties were still banned and one third of each district committee was appointed by the Rawlings government. Ghana is divided into ten regions, each with its own regional council.

THE JUDICIARY

The judicial system, which is based on English legal practice, remains unchanged. In addition to statutory laws there are customary laws and the English structure of common law, which is a series of laws not written down but accepted by the legal system. The superior courts are the Supreme Court, the Court of Appeal, and the High Court, while the lesser courts are the circuit courts, district courts, and juvenile courts. Dissolved for a time during military rule, the Supreme Court has been reestablished as the court of final appeal. Another court outside this system investigates corruption and abuse of public office.

Ashanti notables at a political rally. The power of the tribal chiefs is restricted to tribal matters and customs. They can enact bylaws as long as they do not contradict state laws. They adjudicate on matters of land and inheritance, and organize and are the center of traditional festivals. Whenever local initiatives such as digging wells or land clearance are needed they are organized and overseen by the local chiefs.

TRIBAL GOVERNMENT

The traditional system of government in Ghana has outlasted many military and civilian governments as well as British rule. In ancient times each tribe had its own ruler who dominated life in his own area, often as small as a few villages but sometimes extending across the country. The tribal chief ruled with the help of a council of elders and could call on the loyalty of the villages that he administered in time of war. Below this ruler were a series of local and village chiefs who sat on his council of elders and could depose a bad chief if they chose. The British used the tribal chieftaincies to maintain control during colonial times, and the system remains in place today. Before the British came, the tribal chief had power over all aspects of life and law. The British accepted the chiefs' rule over tribal matters but sat as a court of appeal when tribal disputes threatened to turn into war. Since independence in 1957 the various governments have retained this system, while gradually reducing its power.

After 1957, regional houses of chiefs were set up, which elected representatives to sit in a national House of Chiefs. A ministry was set up to oversee tribal matters such as land rights and the appointment, removal, and succession of new chiefs. Even a judicial system has been used to adjudicate in disputes between individuals and their chiefs.

One unusual tribal chief of Ghana is Lynne Symonds, a schoolteacher from Norfolk in Britain, who was made a chief of the Mamprugipuigi-naba tribe in 1996 after organizing aid to the poverty-stricken villages of northern Ghana.

A member of Ghana's police force.

THE ARMY

Since 1957 the army has played a leading role in the government of Ghana. For 25 years the army was responsible for many coups: all have been relatively popular and targeted at corrupt civil governments. The army is comparatively small. There are 7,000 troops in the armed forces and only 0.7% of GNP (gross national product) is spent on the military, compared to a world average of 3.7%.

GHANA'S FIRST LEADER

Like current president, Jerry Rawlings, Kwame Nkrumah, Ghana's first prime minister, was a powerful and popular leader. He was born in 1909 in the British Gold Coast colony. After teaching in the British colony for some years, Nkrumah left for Lincoln University in the United States, to study politics, particularly Marx, Lenin, and Marcus Garvey, the 1920s Jamaican American leader. He returned to the Gold Coast in 1947 at the invitation of the United Gold Coast Convention (UGCC), a party agitating for independence.

He became very popular, addressing meetings all over the country. In 1948, after several riots, Nkrumah was briefly arrested. Later he split with the UGCC, which he considered too middle-class, and founded a new party based on the principle of immediate self-government, the Convention People's Party (CPP). In 1950 he orchestrated a series of demonstrations, strikes, and noncooperation activities. In the ensuing civil disruption, Nkrumah was arrested a second time and sentenced to a year's imprisonment.

In 1951, while still in jail, Nkrumah was elected to parliament in a massive demonstration of political support, and in 1952 he became prime minister of the Gold Coast. He served as prime minister for five years under British rule and oversaw the peaceful changeover to independence. His style of government then changed. Soon he began to imprison people without trial. Nevertheless, his public building programs made him popular with ordinary people. In 1960 he became president of the Republic of Ghana under Ghana's second constitution.

Always interested in Black African politics, Nkrumah began to champion the idea of African unity—a single, massive, African state. His development projects grew more and more expensive and unrealistic, and soon Ghana was in debt to foreign powers. As dissent grew, Nkrumah began to exert his political control in an increasingly draconian way. In 1962 an attempt was made on his life, and he withdrew from public view. Ghana became a one-party state, and food shortages made life hard for the ordinary people. While on a visit to Beijing in 1966, Nkrumah was deposed by the police and army. He died in exile in 1972.

FOREIGN POLICY

Ghana's foreign policy has emphasized good relations with its neighbors. There is close coordination of currencies, trade, infrastructure, and education with its close neighbor Burkina Faso. Nigeria, Togo, and Côte d'Ivoire all harbor economic and political refugees from Ghana. In 1983 Nigeria expelled a million Ghanaians, causing a serious crisis in an already struggling economy. Coups in Ghana and Togo have been blamed on each country's political refugees. Although Ghana practices a market economy, relations with the United States are cool. Nevertheless, the United States provides economic aid to Ghana. Ghana has also come under criticism from Amnesty International over arrests of political dissidents.

ECONOMY

IN RECENT YEARS GHANA HAS ENJOYED one of the healthiest economies in Africa. After independence Ghana's economy suffered greatly at the hands of rulers with grandiose schemes and corrupt administrations. From the strongest economy in 1957 it became one of the poorest countries in Africa. Nkrumah's policy of nationalization, huge expenditures on projects such as the Akosombo Dam, as well as alignment with eastern European countries resulted in a serious decline in production and a drop in per capita income. The military governments and ineffective civilian rule that followed worsened the situation. The stability of the Rawlings years and tough economic policies have helped reverse Ghana's decline and sparked renewed foreign interest in investing in the country.

Ghana has traditionally been rich in natural resources, especially gold. Industries based on these resources are back in production. The Rawlings administration sought the help of the International Monetary Fund, which

Opposite: **Farm workers in a tree nursery.**

Left: **Takoradi container port. More than a million tons (900,000 metric tons) of cargo pass through Takoradi every year.**

A billboard urges Ghanaians to export more.

recommended an economic recovery program aimed at a free-market economy, tight control of spending, and the removal of subsidies for staple foods. Although unpopular, these measures have won acceptance.

Ghana's economy is based on agriculture and mining, and its chief exports are gold and cocoa. Accra has become the main artery through which Ghana's exports are moved and luxury commodities enter the country.

Many African countries are producers of primary products, such as minerals and crops, and their wellbeing depends on world commodity prices that are controlled by markets far away in the international financial centers. Prices can fall and wipe out a country's income. In the mid-1960s cocoa prices collapsed, pushing Ghana's economy into serious decline.

AGRICULTURE

Besides cocoa, Ghana also produces bananas, cola nuts, citrus fruit, coconuts, rice, palm fruit, tobacco, and shea butter. Bananas were first exported from Ghana in 1929. They are grown in the southeast, in the forested region where the weather is warm and humid. Banana production is difficult because the fruit is delicate and easily damaged. It has to be picked while unripe and kept in special cool containers. Fortunately in Ghana, the growing areas are near the southern sea ports, so the bananas can be transported quickly and are less likely to suffer damage.

Cola nuts, the basic ingredient of the many cola drinks consumed around the world, are a lucrative industry in Ghana. The trees they grow on need the same environment as cocoa, so the two crops compete for the same available space on most farms. Cola trees, however, grow faster and are used as shade trees for young cocoa plants, so the two plants are often seen growing together.

Farmers till the soil in northern Ghana. Agriculture accounts for about 50% of Ghana's gross national product (GNP) and employs almost half the working population.

The shea tree grows wild in Ghana. It produces shea butter, which is used in the manufacture of soap, candles, and some foods.

Workers crate tomatoes near Kumasi.

Coconuts are grown along the coast. They were first grown commercially after 1920 when the colonial government set up plantations and nurseries and distributed seedlings to local farmers to encourage the crop. The main product of coconut trees is copra, the dried meat of its fruit. Tobacco is one of the smallest cash crops in Ghana. It has been grown commercially since the 1930s and is cultivated in small pockets in various parts of the country. A tobacco company was established in Ghana in 1951.

Sugarcane is grown mostly on a small scale by individual farmers; there are few commercial sugarcane plantations in Ghana. The plant needs enough rainfall to thrive and is therefore grown in valleys or in the forested region. Cultivated mostly for domestic consumption, it is also used by the alcohol industry. Factories sited near plantations convert the juice to sugar.

Besides these commercial products, many other crops are grown and either consumed within the villages or sold at local markets. They include corn, millet, groundnuts, tomatoes, green vegetables, peppers, cocoyam (a root vegetable), cassava, yams, and plantains.

COCOA

Cocoa is Ghana's most important cash crop and its highest export earner, accounting for about two-thirds of the country's revenue. It provides employment to more than half a million people. It also provided much of the capital for Ghana's many infrastructure projects. Cocoa was first exported in 1885, and in 1890 the colonial government set up a botanical garden to raise seedlings to distribute to local farmers. It is cultivated mostly in forested regions because it needs deep, well-drained soil and a high rainfall throughout the year. Too much rain at any one time can encourage disease in the plant.

The crop is first cultivated on forest land that has been cleared of all but a few trees; these shade the young plants. Additional shade comes from cocoyams and plantains, which also help provide some income while the cocoa trees are small. The trees become productive after about five years and at this stage the work becomes labor-intensive. Harvesting, which can take three or four months, begins in September. The large, ripe pods are collected and the beans scooped out and fermented for several days. They are then sun-dried for about two weeks and packed into bags for shipment.

Fish are often sun-dried or smoked for local consumption. Ghana also has a tuna canning industry aimed at the export market.

FISHING AND LIVESTOCK

Fishing is a small domestic industry. Families along the coast go out in canoes to catch fish to supplement their diet. Larger commercial boats are motorized and use nets to catch tuna, bream, and herring. A state fishing agency operates a fleet of trawlers, and there are some private foreign-owned fishing fleets. In the north of the country a few small fish farms exist. Lake Volta provides another useful supply of freshwater fish. The many lagoons along the coast are another source of seafood. Tema is Ghana's largest fishing port.

Cattle are commercially reared on a small scale in the coastal savanna areas such as the Accra Plains. The total head of cattle reared, however, falls far short of demand, and about 60% of the beef consumed in Ghana is imported. The drier northern region is ideal for raising cattle, but in that region cattle traditionally represent wealth. Therefore, thousands of cattle are kept but not for meat, being too valuable to eat. Raising cattle is difficult in many areas because of seasonal water shortages and because no fodder crop is grown.

MANUFACTURING

Countries that have developed manufacturing industries have far more stable economies than countries that depend on primary production. World prices of manufactured goods are more stable than those of staples. But establishing a manufacturing base is expensive and risky, with high outlays in infrastructure, research and development, training the workforce, and a much more complex administration for manufactured goods. When Ghana was a colony, all primary products were exported to Britain and processed there. After independence both local entrepreneurs and the various governments realized the importance of developing a manufacturing base, but by 1960 only 8.6% of the working population were engaged in manufacturing.

The Rawlings government has created a conducive climate for investment; as a result manufacturing has grown by about 9% a year. By the 1990s manufacturing amounted to 14% of the GNP. Ghana's food processing industries include sugar refineries, flour mills, and several cocoa processing factories where Ghanaian chocolate is made.

A textile printing factory in Tema.

The country also has a beef processing plant, milk processing factories, vegetable-oil mills that produce coconut and palm oil, and small tomato and pineapple factories. There are several breweries making beer from imported hops, a soft drink industry, and cigarette factories.

Cotton grown in Ghana as well as imported fibers are processed into cloth and then into clothes in factories around the southern cities. Jute, kenaf, and roselle are fiber plants grown in Ghana that are processed into cloth, rope, and sacks in small factories.

The forestry industry supports sawmills, furniture and boat building, and the manufacture of plywood and paper products. Ghana also has oil refineries that process kerosene, gasoline, and diesel fuel; cement works and brick factories using imported materials; and chemical plants that make insecticides, paints, and pharmaceuticals.

ELECTRICITY

Before 1966 when the Akosombo hydroelectric plant was opened, electricity was produced by small diesel generators. The new power plant supplied electricity to Accra and the towns of southern Ghana. Most of its power went to the aluminum smelting plant nearby and for several years the power supply was inadequate because of operating problems and a series of droughts.

Since 1981 the system has been improved and extended. Now most major towns receive electricity.

The Akosombo Dam enables Ghana to supply electricity to neighboring countries and earn foreign exchange.

MINING AND FORESTRY

Gold, diamonds, manganese, and bauxite are mined in Ghana. Gold mining slumped after independence, but has recently begun to catch up with cocoa as a leading export. Ghana's diamonds are mostly of industrial quality. Ghana is also the world's eighth largest producer of manganese, with mines in the western region. There are large reserves of bauxite in Ghana, but mining is as yet undeveloped and most of the raw material used is imported. In recent years foreign companies have shown an increasing interest in Ghana's mineral resources. A small amount of offshore oil has also been discovered, but it is as yet not enough to make commercial extraction worthwhile.

Ghana's forest reserves have been exploited for many years, particularly during the 1960s. After a decline in production in the 1970s and 1980s, the country's timber resources are again being managed and exports are on the rise. Ghana has sufficient reserves until the year 2030.

Gold miners display a gold bar. The Ashanti goldfields are Ghana's largest producer of gold. Although there is a small gold processing plant in Ghana, the raw material is mostly exported.

Workers construct a new highway in Accra.

TRANSPORTATION

Ghana's chief means of transport are roads, railways, rivers, and air. In the more rural and undeveloped north of the country horses and donkeys are still used. Transportation routes link up the major areas of economic production, connecting them with urban centers and ultimately with Accra. Roads for cars and trucks were first constructed in the early years of the 20th century, first to link the southern towns, and then they were extended to the cocoa plantations in the southwest.

Like much of Ghana's economy, the road system was not maintained during the 1970s and 1980s, but new projects are under way to pave the roads. Asphalt roads run along the coast, joining the coastal towns, and to Kumasi in the center of Ghana and then northward to Tamale. Other similar roads link the other major towns. A two-lane freeway runs from Accra to Tema. Other roads are smaller and unsurfaced and are often swept away in the rainy season, making travel difficult.

MAMMY WAGONS

An essential part of the daily life of Ghanaians is the mammy wagon. Whether going to work, to the market, home to visit the family at festival time, or to the seaside, everyone uses this form of public transportation. Mammy wagons are privately owned and run. They are usually large, five-ton Bedford trucks, with the wooden body covered with a tarpaulin roof and fitted out with wooden benches. They carry passengers and cargo.

They travel around towns or between them, stopping to let people on or off on demand. Each town has its own wagon station where "bookmen" try to collect passengers for their wagons. Trucks leave when they are full. They have a very short life span since most of them are in continual use and travel on dirt roads. While they are in use, they are brightly painted and kept very clean.

Passengers make the best of their rather rough ride. The wagons are meant to carry up to 30 passengers, but often carry far more. A long journey is made more enjoyable with many roadside stops and much gossip along the way. In the towns the mammy wagons are known as *tro tros* ("TRO tros").

Railways extend across the country, linking major production areas with Accra. The railways are largely used to move freight. Schedules are irregular so the trains are unpopular as public transportation. Many of Ghana's rivers are not navigable but the dam at Akosombo has created a huge lake that makes water transportation from the north convenient and inexpensive. Ports have been built around the lake to facilitate this increasingly popular mode of travel.

Ghana has small airports at Takoradi, Kumasi, Sunyani, and Tamale, in addition to the Kotoka international airport in Accra.

GHANAIANS

ABOUT 16.5 MILLION PEOPLE live in Ghana, belonging to over 50 different ethnic groups, each with its own language and customs. For all those differences, Ghana is a nation of ethnic harmony, with very few instances of conflict brought about by cultural differences.

The Akan tribes form the largest ethnic group in Ghana, making up about 52% of the population. The Akan are not a single ethnic group, and they speak many dialects of their common language, Twi. These tribes live mainly in the southern half of the country.

The northern tribes are more diverse and make up about 30% of the population. They have different, unrelated languages, but speak the common tongue, Dagbane. The Ewe tribes live in the Volta region and make up about 10% of the population. The Ga-Adangme tribes, who make up 8% of the population, live mostly in the coastal area around Accra.

The other major division between the people of Ghana is that of town and country. About 65% of the population live in the country, while 35% live in the cities. This division is changing continually in favor of city life, as more and more people take up manufacturing and commercial jobs rather than agricultural ones. About 45% of the population are designated economically active, meaning that they take part in the market economy rather than carry out subsistence farming. About 40% of the working population are in agriculture, while 23% are in service industries. The average family size is comparatively low for Africa, at 4.9 people per household.

Opposite and above: **Ghana has a young population, with 46% of the population under the age of 15 and only 13% over 45.**

*Because the
symbol of a chief's
power is the stool
he sits on, getting
rid of a bad or
unpopular chief
is called
"destooling."*

**Knife grinders waiting for
customers.**

Ghana does not have the social distinctions based on class or wealth that exist in many European countries. It is essentially an egalitarian society with a tribal structure. Within the tribe all men are equal, however rich they are, although in some tribes only certain families can become chiefs. But the chiefs are chosen by the people, who can "destool" or remove an unpopular chief.

In many of the tribes property and land are owned by families, not individuals, and is continually redistributed around the family so few people ever build up large personal fortunes or estates. Conversely, few people are really destitute or without family to support them because everyone has a tribe or clan they can count on in times of trouble.

THE AKAN

The Akan tribes, the largest ethnic group in Ghana, live in the southwest and central areas of the country. Subgroups within the Akan group include the Brong, Banda, Adanse, Assin, Twifo, Denkyera, Akyem, Wassa, Akwamu, and Ashanti. The Akan tribes originally lived in the savanna areas in the northwest of Ghana and the northeast of Côte d'Ivoire. They traded cola nuts and gold, which they panned from the rivers, with the people of the coast. They all speak various dialects of the Twi language. Their lives today are still organized around village communities, with the majority surviving on subsistence farming. Nevertheless, many have migrated to the towns and taken up a modern, urban lifestyle.

A subgroup of the Akan are the Fanti, who live on the southern coast between Accra and Sekondi-Takoradi. Their oral tradition claims that they moved to the coast from the Ashanti region in the 17th century. They grow cassava, cocoyam, and plantains. Many also have small commercial ventures in cocoa, palm oil, and timber.

Ashanti schoolgirls near Kumasi.

The Fanti live in single-walled homesteads. Many have migrated to the coast and reside in other West African countries, living off fishing.

A Fulani girl.

THE NORTHERN TRIBES

The Dagomba are one of the major tribes in the north. They are believed to have migrated from east of Lake Chad, across modern Nigeria, and into their present homeland in the north central region of Ghana. The Dagomba speak a Niger-Congo language and are farmers, growing yam, sorghum, millet, corn, and groundnuts. They also raise cattle and other livestock, and live in walled villages. They are among the least affected by modern life.

The Mamprusi are another tribe living in the north of Ghana. They inhabit the area between the Nasia River and the White Volta. The Mamprusi speak several different dialects of the Ga language. They live in circular compounds in areas of vegetation known as orchard bush, and are farmers, cultivating crops such as millet, corn, hibiscus, rice, and tobacco. Like the Dagomba, their songs tell of a time when they lived near Lake Chad and migrated to Ghana.

Another tribe, the Guan, also speak Ga. They live in the area where the Black Volta and White Volta merge. Strangely, in this tribe the rulers speak a different language than the ordinary people. The Guan live in small villages of less than 300 people and practice shifting cultivation, farming a piece of land until it is barren, and then moving on.

The Fulani are a nomadic tribe who live throughout West Africa. They speak Fulfulde. Those in Ghana are chiefly herdsmen, looking after the herds of other northern tribes.

OTHER TRIBES

The Ewe live in southeastern Ghana as well as in Benin and the southern half of Togo. Their original home was in modern Benin, but they were driven out by the expansion of the Yoruba empire in the 16th century. They speak a version of the Kwa language and are farmers and fishermen as well as potters and blacksmiths.

The Ga also live in southeastern Ghana. They are coastal people, speaking a version of the Kwa language. They arrived in Ghana in the 17th century, making their way down the Niger River and across the Volta. They established the towns of Accra, Osu, Labadi, Teshi, Nunga, and Tema, each with a stool as its symbol of leadership. Originally farmers, the Ga have branched out into fishing and trade. Unusually among Ghanaians, the main breadwinner in the family is the woman.

Speaking very similar dialects are another group of tribes called the Adangme. They live along the Volta and part of the coast. They are farmers, growing millet, cassava, yams, corn, plantain, and some cash crops.

DRESS

In cities of southern Ghana the typical dress is Western-style, with shorts and T-shirts for men or a suit and tie for businessmen. Women wear dresses or pants cut from imported, patterned cloth or local traditional designs. Often the cotton cloth is made in Europe but has pictures of Ghanaian political leaders on it. The women wear the cloth to honor their leaders.

An Ewe woman in traditional dress. Unlike most of the other tribes of Ghana, the Ewe never formed a single central state.

A woman in *kente* dress.

The traditional cloth of Ghana is called *kente* cloth. Narrow strips of cloth are woven on small looms and sewn together by hand to make several yards of material. Each pattern printed on the cloth has a story and significance for the various tribes. Women in the cities may have their *kente* cloth made into dresses, skirts, and blouses.

Traditional styles of dress vary from region to region. In the north are many Muslims and their style of dress reflects their religious beliefs. Men wear loose-flowing, full-length robes, usually blue, white, or a dark color.

In the south the cloth is brightly colored and patterned. A man's traditional dress is made of 26–33 feet (8–10 m) of cloth draped in a very specific way and often worn over a shirt and shorts. At funerals the appropriate color to wear is red.

Women's traditional dress consists of three pieces of cloth. The first is a loose blouse. The second is a large piece of cloth wrapped around the waist, forming a floor-length skirt. The blouse is tucked into the girdle, which holds up the skirt. Above this the woman wraps the third of her garments, which is tied around the waist, and then folded over the left shoulder. This third piece can be used to carry a baby. Most women wear some form of headdress, either a scarf tied simply around the head or a more elaborately designed turban.

KOFI ANNAN

Kofi Annan, a Ghanaian, became very well-known in 1997 when he was made the United Nations secretary-general. His term of office began with a crisis in Iraq, where UN weapons inspectors were in dispute with the Iraqi government over access to certain areas. Annan was able to defuse what might have developed into a very dangerous situation, with American and British troops poised to attack Iraq.

Annan is a career official in the United Nations. He joined the World Health Organization in 1962 as a clerk in Geneva and after 30 years of service, was nominated to its highest position. He was educated in the United States and Switzerland. His job at the United Nations comes at a time of crisis for the organization. Its role is no longer well-defined in a post-Cold War era, and it is seriously in debt, with about half the member states not paying their contribution to its upkeep. The United States owes over one billion US dollars. Annan has five years as secretary-general, with the possibility of a further five-year term.

KINGSLEY OFUSU

In October 1992 nine young Ghanaian boys from Takoradi decided to seek their fortune in the West and stowed away on a boat called the *MC Ruby*. Four days from Le Havre in France the stowaways were discovered by the Ukrainian crew and taken out on deck and shot, and their bodies were thrown into the sea. One of them, who had head injuries, escaped from the crew and spent four days being hunted around the ship. Once in Le Havre he escaped and reported the deaths of his brother and his friends to the authorities.

After a long trial, the Ukrainian crew were sentenced to life imprisonment. The survivor, Kingsley Ofusu, was offered a chance to stay in France and study engineering. That might have been the end of a tragic affair, except that American actor Danny Glover heard the story and decided to make a movie about Ofusu's experiences. The rights to his story made Ofusu a wealthy man by Ghanaian standards, and he became both rich and famous because of his terrible ordeal. The Ghanaian premiere of the movie, called *Deadly Voyage*, raised the money to build a rehabilitation center in Takoradi to help the many returned stowaways who have had less horrific experiences than Ofusu, but who nevertheless failed to make their fortune in the West.

LIFESTYLE

GHANA HAS SEEN TREMENDOUS CHANGE in social structures and lifestyles in the 20th century. In many rural areas the threads that once held society together have altered as Ghanaians move away from a subsistence economy to a managed economy. In the cities wealth, migration, education, and new expectations have led to a society based on the nuclear family, rather than the clan. Enormous differences in wealth, education, healthcare, housing, and opportunities exist in the country.

The changes brought about in economic policy by the Rawlings government have improved the lives of many, particularly those in the south and those employed in manufacturing and trade. But life remains hard for others, especially in the far north, where drought has brought extreme poverty and malnutrition. Several charities operate in Ghana. One of them is Actionaid, which works mainly in the north of the country, providing loans, seed, education, and healthcare.

Opposite: **Women balance loads of calabashes on their way to the market.**

Left: **Mothers carry their children the traditional way.**

A family weeds their corn field.

TRADITIONAL SOCIAL STRUCTURES

The old tribal structures are still very important in the rural areas. The simplest unit of social structure, the extended family, usually has a man as its head. He has responsibilities not only within his extended family, but also in the village in which they live—perhaps peacekeeping, organizing a festival, making sure spiritual observances are carried out, or looking after the water supply or sanitation. He forms part of the village's council of elders that advises the village chief on the running of the village.

In turn the village chief sits on the council of elders of the divisional chief. A division might be a series of villages. Divisional chiefs advise the paramount chief, who is the highest authority in the tribe. The paramount chief, like the other, lesser chiefs under him, inherits his position through his family, but he can be rejected by his people in favor of a relative if he is an ineffective leader. In the north of the country the chief's symbol of power is an animal skin, while in the south it is a stool.

Ashanti elders wear gold
on their heads during a
festival.

When they become chief they are "enstooled" or "enskinned," and if they are removed from office, they are "destooled" or "deskinned." Ordinary citizens can never become chief. Successive national governments have never sought to interfere with the chieftaincies. At the regional level the paramount chiefs meet in a body set up by the government called the regional house of chiefs. Regional houses elect representatives to sit in a national house of chiefs. When disputes between paramount chiefs occur, a judicial committee made up of chiefs and a high court judge adjudicates.

Each paramount chief and his elders can make bylaws regarding traditional matters. They arbitrate on tribal matters, such as land tenure, inheritance, and custom. They are the essential core of all festivals that take place in Ghana. Although they have no legal role in local government matters, their disapproval of a new project or local government law would ensure that it did not operate. The paramount chiefs embody all that is best in their tribe. On important occasions they wear beautiful clothing and gold and silver jewelry.

An extended family in northern Ghana.

THE FAMILY

The most common traditional family unit in Ghana is matrilineal, where a person is related to everyone on the mother's side of the family, including the mother's brothers, sisters, nieces, nephews, aunts, and uncles. In rural areas the matrilineal family often lives in one compound or neighborhood and shares the land and property communally. Such an extended family would be called a clan. In Ghana it is known as *abusa* ("ah-BOO-sah").

Less common are patrilineal families, where the family or clan is made up of those on the father's side. Included in the family are the spirits of dead family members. At the head of the family is the chief, the man who sits with the village elders and carries out the tribal duties. In a small village all the residents may be from one family. When a chief is deposed or dies, all the sons of the women in his family if of the next generation are possible candidates for his position. The mothers in the family are thus important and powerful, especially the mother of the chief.

The clan system affects every aspect of the Ghanaian lifestyle. Land tenure is held by the family, including the dead ancestors, so land is rarely sold. Every member of an *abusa* has equal rights to the resources of the clan; likewise, any individual wealth belongs to their family. The clan system also affects how public works are carried out in villages. If a new well or schoolroom is needed, it will belong to the whole *abusa*. Everyone therefore lends a hand or, if they can, donates cash to the building work.

URBAN SOCIAL STRUCTURES

The clan system is less obvious in urban areas. Many people have migrated to the towns, leaving their clan behind. They earn a salary and live in nuclear families. If they are able to save they will use the money to put their children through school, or buy household goods, or even their own house. Their ties to their clan may be a general sense of duty, rather than shared ownership of property. Family size is small.

Villagers chip in to help construct a building.

MARRIAGE

The traditional Ghanaian concept of marriage is very different from the Western one. Arranging the marriage is the father's responsibility, so when the son has chosen a wife he tells his father about his choice. His mother usually checks the suitability of the girl. She might ask neighbors about illnesses in the family and how closely related she is to her future husband.

If she is acceptable, the father begins negotiations. A cryptic message passes between the two fathers, and the girl's family members do their own check on the boy and his background. A message goes back if the boy is found acceptable and the wedding plans begin. By this time the boy's father will have made two payments to the bride's family—one when he sent his preliminary message, called the "knocking fee," and another when the agreement was given. A third payment is the brideprice when the girl is handed over.

The first two fees are negotiated by the bride's father and they become his, but the third fee is a "deposit" that must be handed back in the event of a divorce. Among some tribes other payments go to brothers, aunts, and other relatives to compensate for their loss. Often, for example among the Grusi-speaking tribes in northern Ghana, the payments are in the form of an animal. The marriage ceremony itself, a meeting between the parents to formalize the relationship, may or may not include either bride or groom. The bride is then summoned to the groom's house with her friends and relatives. At the groom's house are his relatives, friends, and musicians. A boisterous party takes place and the girl then stays on at her husband's house.

Among some tribes, particularly the matrilineal ones, the girl often returns to her own family home to live. This is the case among the Fanti, an Akan tribe. Among some groups polygamy is common. The Fulani for example often live in family units of a man and his several wives and their children. Some men may have two families in separate homes, with two sets of children each living with their own mother's clan. Divorce is a matter of paying back the brideprice. The goods that the husband gave to the wife's family need not be returned.

Opposite: **A young couple in Western dress at their wedding.**

MARRIAGE GIFTS

When a couple marries many expenses are involved besides the brideprice and the wedding party. The husband must give his wife gifts to bring to the marriage. These might be furniture (such as a chest of drawers), sets of clothing, shoes, perfume, and money. The wife must bring her share of possessions to the marriage.

She already has the possessions she was given at puberty, but must add to these domestic utensils, such as buckets, pots, dishes, towels, and other small items, as well as the food for the first week of their marriage. These gifts are exchanged before the wedding is finalized, and it is only on acceptance of these gifts that the marriage goes ahead. If either partner fails to provide his or her proper share, the marriage can be canceled.

CHILDREN

The clan system has greatly influenced family size. If a clan was to be strong, the next generation had to be large. In the past each couple was encouraged to have as many children as possible. As many as 13 births was common for each woman, although many of the babies would not survive. Tribal wars and slave raids took more children. Nowadays, with land becoming scarcer, more children means a smaller share for each member of the clan. Tribal wars have ended, the infant mortality rate has declined, education is expensive, and family planning is available. Clans therefore think less of having many children and more about providing for a few.

Even so, children are still seen as an economic and social asset to the clan. In their work for the family they repay the cost of their birth and upbringing. Children fetch water, sweep the yard, tidy the house, prepare meals, wash, and help on the farm. Girls have the toughest workload, helping on the farm, doing the housework, and cooking for the family.

Boys are treated more casually, being allowed time to play. In poor families boys are expected to contribute to the family income. Besides using a slingshot to catch birds, they might do some gardening for pay. The more enterprising boys have a small business of their own at a market. If they can collect enough money they can buy paraffin or snacks and sell them at a profit. Children as young as 6 years of age may have such jobs in the evening after school.

When children grow up their obligation to their parents continues. If they have moved to the town they are expected to send money home regularly. If they still live in the village they must provide for their parents. They must also meet their funeral expenses.

COMING OF AGE IN GHANA

Coming of age is an important part of life for village children. It marks their arrival at adulthood and is celebrated by the whole village. It is usually incorporated into one of the festivals celebrated by the village.

Boys are given the uniform of their local militia. The night before the festival a bonfire is lit and the young boys to be initiated and their fathers gather together. They are taught the secret stories of their militia and cleansing rituals are carried out. At puberty all boys undergo circumcision.

Ceremonies for girls are more elaborate, with rituals varying according to the customs of the tribe. Generally they follow the pattern that on reaching puberty the girls are taken out to the family compound and put on display for all the neighbors to see. In some tribes the girls wear very little besides beads. In others they walk around the streets, greeting the neighbors. After this there is an eight-day period when the girls are isolated and cannot touch anything associated with adult life, such as the stove, their newly bought clothes, or the gifts that their family and neighbors bring. At the end of this period of exclusion the girls are dressed in their finest clothes and presented with the gifts that form their capital and that remain theirs even after marriage.

Downtown Kumasi. Car ownership even in the cities is low, and less than 1% of the total population owns a car.

THE LIVING ENVIRONMENT

The cities offer a variety of homes to suit different budgets. There are government housing projects as well as estates of privately owned houses that would not look out of place in an American city. The home of a typical city dweller is likely to have electricity, plumbing, good sanitation, and consumer goods such as a TV set, refrigerator, or perhaps even a video recorder. Western-style upholstered armchairs and carpets may fill the rooms. The wealthiest people in Ghana have lifestyles that are comparable to that of their counterparts in the West.

In other parts of the city, such as Nima in Accra, are slums or shantytowns. These are unplanned areas with no piped water, electricity, or sanitation. Often open sewers flow through the streets. In Accra, 700,000 people have no access to sanitation. Many of those who live in the shantytowns are migrants who have no clan system to support them, no financial resources, and no land to grow their food. They mostly live from hand to mouth.

In the countryside the traditional house is built by its owner out of the cheapest available materials. No planning permission is required, nor are there rules about sanitation. A typical village house of someone who is well-off has several rooms, including a kitchen, bathroom, living room, and verandahs, where most of the day's activities take place.

Each parent may have their own bedroom, with communal rooms for the young girls and individual rooms for teenage girls and all the boys. Typical household furniture may include carved stools that are kept indoors, with some chairs and rougher-made wooden stools outside. The bedrooms may have a simple wooden bed with a mattress and a sheet. Floors are covered in reed mats. Clothes and possessions are kept in chests. Children sleep on rush mats that are aired outdoors every day.

In the village one may find the village well, the elementary school, a church or mosque, perhaps a bar, and a few public buildings, such as a mill, a dispensary and clinic, and a marketplace. Beyond the village are the fields, where the crops are grown and animals grazed.

A village in central Ghana. If a family needs a new house, everyone helps to build it. Most village houses are made of mud, or "swish" as it is called in Ghana.

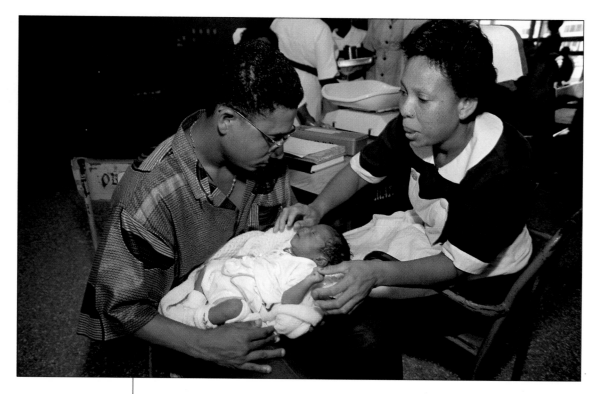

A newborn baby at an Accra hospital. The infant mortality rate in Ghana, though among the lowest in Africa, is high by world standards at 73 deaths per 1,000. There is one doctor for every 23,500 people and one hospital bed for every 638.

HEALTH

Some parts of Ghana experience long periods of either torrential rain with flooding or severe drought. Water management is thus an important aspect of the nation's healthcare. About half the rural population do not have access to safe drinking water. Many people draw their water from a nearby river, which may be polluted by insecticides, the runoff from a factory upstream, or animal waste. Where complex water systems have been installed, such as piped water from a well, the local community may not have the means or skills to maintain it and the supply is lost.

Most rural women in Ghana depend on traditional midwives for help during their confinement. Many of these midwives have now been trained in nutrition for expectant mothers as well as basic hygiene. Charities, the churches, and the government have also established clinics in many villages, where vaccination programs are carried out and rudimentary healthcare provided. For more serious illnesses people must travel to the urban areas, where most of the government hospitals are located.

EDUCATION

Compared to many of its African neighbors, Ghana has a good educational system, with six years of free and compulsory elementary education for all children from ages 6 to 12. Children must provide their own textbooks and materials, which some parents cannot afford. In rural areas facilities can be as basic as a shady spot under a tree. Often teachers are difficult to recruit for poor and remote locations. They are usually posted from another part of Ghana and are not part of the local clan, so they may feel excluded and find life quite hard. For the first three years education is in the mother tongue and English is taught as a second language. Subsequently, English becomes the official medium of instruction.

About 7% of the elementary school-age population do not attend school. After elementary school, those who can afford it go to secondary school, where fees must be paid. Although Ghanaians value education highly, about 25% of children drop out at this stage because their parents cannot afford the cost or because the children themselves must work and contribute to the family income. In rural Ghana many girls see their future in marriage and drop out of school at an early age. Many parents see little need for an expensive secondary education for a girl who will marry before age 20 and take up farming and child-rearing.

In addition to the state educational system there are a number of private schools. An important feature of the government's efforts to establish literacy in the country are mass education campaigns that make use of the radio to teach literacy, healthcare, good farming practice, and house building.

Secondary schoolchildren discuss a class project. After secondary school a student can go to a vocational or commercial college or a senior secondary school. Students who do not want a university education might choose to attend a teacher-training college. Ghana has five universities, including one near Accra, a university of science and technology at Kumasi, and the University of Cape Coast, which specializes in teacher training.

RELIGION

GHANA HAS MANY RELIGIOUS BELIEFS AND CUSTOMS and almost all Ghanaians practice one religion or another. It is a secular state, so the government does not favor or support any religion over another. The three main religions in Ghana are Christianity, Islam, and animism. Of these, animism is the indigenous religion, while Christianity and Islam are introduced religions.

Many people practice both animism and one of the introduced religions, so figures vary. About 62% of the population are believed to be Christians—30% Protestant, 18% Catholic, and 14% other Christian churches. About 16% of the population is Muslim, with half of these following the Ahmadhiyah branch of that faith. Generally more people in the north are Muslim, while more people in the south are Christian.

Opposite: **A fetish house in the Volta region.**

Left: **Ewe voodooists in Cape Coast.**

TRADITIONAL BELIEFS

Many religions are included in the term "animist" in Ghana. These religions have in common the idea that there is a spiritual world in which things such as trees, rocks, streams, or even the village well, are imbued with life and are able to cause harm or good to people who come in contact with them. Consequently all objects must be treated carefully and appeased if necessary. They can also be called on for help using a juju priest as an intermediary.

Most of Ghana's tribes believe in three forms of spiritual power—the spirits of the things around them, the spirits of their ancestors, and a single god who created the world. The creator god is less important in the immediate lives of the animist tribespeople than the other two. Ancestors are the most important aspect of spiritual life, and the most recently deceased are the most powerful. If properly treated, the ancestors are benevolent. But they can be vengeful if they are slighted—for example, by an improperly conducted ritual.

THE JUJU PRIEST

A mixture of doctor and priest, the juju priest mediates between his patients or congregation and the spirits. The job is often hereditary, with the father passing his skills on to the son. Often the son will have given some sign of his potential, perhaps by falling into a trance. The priest has a wide range of natural herbs and remedies for all kinds of illnesses. Because he may believe that the illness is caused by some malevolent spirit, part of his cure may be to appease that angry spirit or to wear a talisman as protection against it.

A talisman or fetish is made of items that are believed to hold magical power. Often they are made of animal bone or skin. To obtain help from the fetish priest, the suffering person and their family must visit the priest, bringing gifts. The priest listens to their problems and then works his magic to the drumming, singing, and dancing of his assistant priests. He is well paid for the work he does. The more powerful an object was in life, the more power it has to protect the victim, so often the fetish will be part of a tiger or some other powerful creature.

The Mamprusi and Dagomba of northern Ghana believe in the ancestors and also in an earth spirit, whose shrines are in sacred places. Many of these people are also Muslim.

FETISH HOUSES

In the Ashanti religion the supreme deity is called Nyame. Below him are a pantheon of lesser gods embodied by the earth's physical features, such as the Tano River, Nyame's favorite son. Below them are even smaller gods or *abosom* ("ah-BOH-som")—this, translated, is "fetish," an object of spiritual power or the power that it represents. While Nyame is so remote that he cannot be appealed to, the *abosom* are ready to help if appealed to in the right way. All over Ghana fetish houses exist where the *abosom* are worshiped and addressed as if they were elders of the tribe. Inside the house is a brass basin containing the essential elements of the *abosom*—perhaps some river mud, herbs, beads, shells, or other revered objects. The fetish house becomes the home of the *abosom*, which can enter into the body of a priest if it so wishes.

AKAN BELIEFS

Like the ancient Greeks, the Ewe believe in a creator god called Mawu as well as a pantheon of lesser gods. They also worship their ancestors. Many of them have adopted Christianity, which they practice alongside their other beliefs.

The Akan people, who make up the largest group in Ghana, believe that a person is made up of two parts—a spiritual part and a physical part. Each person inherits their physical being, called the *bogya* ("BOG-yah," or blood), from their mother and their spiritual side, or *nton* ("n-TON"), from the father. The Akan have their own calendar, which consists of nine cycles of 40 days, called *adae* ("AHD-ay"). In each cycle there are two special days when the tribe pays its respects to the spirits of the ancestors.

The Akan maintain the stools of past chiefs, believing that their souls rest in the stools. So in each 40-day period a day is set aside when the stools are worshiped. The stool room is usually a sacred place that only the chief and the priests of the ancestors can enter. In some tribes ordinary people are never allowed to see the stools, even when they are taken outside for purification rites. During the day of worship the stools are visited by the chief and his attendants and are given food and drink, and the chief retells the stories of the ancestors' brave deeds.

THE SUPREME BEING

An Akan story tells of how the supreme creator got into the sky. In the very earliest days the creator lived close to man, on the rooftops of the houses. One day he was passing some old women pounding *fufu* ("FOO-foo"). The harder the women pounded, the farther Nyame flew into the sky until eventually he reached the highest heavens and decided to stay there. But now he was no longer close to the people that he created, so he had to call on the tallest things to talk to his people for him. That is how people learned to worship the high things, such as mountains and trees, which were close to Nyame and could carry messages to him. When the Ashanti create altars to Nyame it is always a tree with a fetish figure sitting in it. When a drum maker or boat builder cuts down a tree to make his drum or boat he always propitiates the tree because of its power to intercede between him and the supreme being.

CHRISTIANITY

The first Christians to come to Ghana were the Portuguese, who introduced Roman Catholicism in the 15th century. They made little effort to convert the local people, so Christianity did not take root until the second half of the 18th century, when missionary societies began to set up schools and churches.

The Basel Missionary Society started missionary work in Ghana in 1828. The Wesleyan Methodists arrived in the 1830s, led by Thomas Birch Freeman. He was half-African and went to the Ashanti region to set up his mission. By 1843 the Wesleyans had 21 missions in Ghana, and in 1876 they founded the first secondary school in Ghana. Farther inland, Bremen missions were set up east of the Volta, working with the Ewe people. This church later became the modern Evangelical Presbyterian Church of Ghana.

In the early years of the 20th century many people converted to Christianity because of the work of William Wade Harris, a Liberian who traveled across West Africa and whose teachings were so powerful that he was deported from Côte d'Ivoire. Although he was an American Episcopalian missionary, he helped convert thousands of people from animism to Methodism, Roman Catholicism, and Anglicanism. His followers in Ghana set up their own church called the Church of the Twelve Apostles. Other Christian churches in Ghana include the Presbyterian, Evangelical, Baptist, African Methodist, and Episcopal Zion churches.

Christians celebrate Easter in Elmina.

Dancing in a village church near Kumasi.

SPIRITUAL CHURCHES

The churches that arrived in Ghana in the 18th and 19th centuries appealed to people because of their similar ideas of a single creator god and also because of their efforts to educate local people. But the imported churches lacked an African flavor, and over the years indigenous churches that mixed the belief in a forgiving savior with the high spirits and enthusiasm of African cultural life began to spring up all across West Africa.

One of these churches was the Church of the Lord, Aladura. This began among the Yoruba people of Nigeria and was based on the ideas of an American church, the Faith Tabernacle Church of Philadelphia, which practiced faith healing and the laying on of hands. In 1918 an influenza epidemic killed many people in West Africa and a prayer group within the Anglican Church began to practice faith healing in an effort to save lives.

By the 1920s this church was forced out of the Anglican Church, but it had become very popular and spread from its home in Nigeria across West Africa, establishing a branch called the Christ Apostolic Church in Ghana. Later churches came to be called Aladura churches and practiced even more unusual forms of Christianity, with prophets who claimed they could foretell the future, heal the sick, and even make amulets for protection, just as the juju priests do. Often these amulets include inscriptions from the Bible rather than pieces of animal bone. Prayer meetings are often very lively, with African-style drumming and street processions.

In Ghana important days in the Christian calendar are Christmas and Good Friday.

ISLAM

Islam arrived in Ghana with Arab traders bringing gold to Sudan, probably sometime around the 17th century. It is more popular among the people in northern Ghana, although there are groups of Muslims throughout the country. Most Fulani, Mamprusi, Dagomba, and some Ashanti have become Muslims.

Islam originated in Arabia in the seventh century and follows the teachings of the Prophet Mohammed. Muslims believe in one God, in angels who bring the word of God to the people, and in the 28 prophets who received God's message. One of these prophets, they believe, was Jesus Christ. Other prophets are Abraham, David, Moses, and the writers of the New Testament, all figures known in Christianity. Muslims also believe in the final day of judgment, when they will hear the trumpet of the angel Asrafil. The form of Islam practiced in Ghana is Sunni Islam, but there is another sect, considered heretical by most other Muslims, which has converts in southern Ghana, called the Ahmadhiyah. This sect recognizes another prophet after Mohammed, a man called Mirza Ghulam Ahmad, who lived in India and claimed to be the *mahdi* ("MAH-dee"), the figure who was to appear at the end of the world. He also claimed to be the reincarnation of Christ and the Hindu god Krishna.

In Ghana the sect is represented by the Telemul Islam Ahmadhiyah Movement, which has its headquarters in Saltpond. It runs several secondary schools and is a proselytizing sect, happy to convert people to any form of Islam, not just its own.

Muslims in northern Ghana perform Friday prayers. Muslims must observe the five pillars of Islam—accept the one true God and Mohammed as his prophet, practice prayer, fast, make a pilgrimage to Mecca during their lifetime, and give alms to the poor.

LANGUAGE

GHANA HAS ABOUT 100 indigenous languages and dialects. In the south these languages tend to be either a form of Twi, Ewe, or Ga, while in the north Dagbane is spoken. The northern and southern languages are not mutually intelligible, so several lingua francas have evolved in the country.

The most widely used is English, which is the official language of Ghana and the medium of instruction in schools. In other areas Hausa, a language from Nigeria, is used for intertribal communication. Most people speak their own mother tongue fluently, understand a few related languages, know a little of the local lingua franca, and would have learned some English in school, which tends to take the form of pidgin English in rural areas. In the cities English is widely spoken, and English-speaking visitors have little difficulty making themselves understood. English is used for all government business, in the business community, for most radio and television broadcasts, and in most publications.

Opposite: **A schoolgirl with her slate.**

Left: **A woman learns to write with the help of an adult literacy worker. About 75% of the male population and about 55% of the female population is literate.**

A policeman talks to a group of street boys.

AKAN LANGUAGES

Most of the people who live along the coast and in the southern regions of Ghana speak an Akan language, mainly Twi-Fanti dialects. The Twi-Fanti dialects are very close, and speakers of these dialects can understand each other well. The vocabulary is the same in most dialects, with differences only in pronunciation and accent. This means that people from the south coast can understand another speaker living as far away as the Black Volta, Lake Volta, or the border with Côte d'Ivoire, although the language they speak may be called Ashanti, Fanti, Akuapem, or any one of tens of other names. Because each language or dialect has a written form, they remain separate languages.

GA LANGUAGES

The people in northern Ghana speak one of three forms of the Ga language—Mole-Dagbane, Grusi, and Gurma. None of these languages is spoken or understood in the south of the country, except by the few people from the north who have migrated south to Accra or one of the other coastal towns. Mole-Dagbane is the most widely spoken branch of the Ga language. It includes the dialects spoken in Nankansi, Gurensi, Dagomba, Mamprusi, and Talensi-Kusasi regions. These languages are not as mutually intelligible as the Twi-Fanti dialects. Neighboring groups understand one another, but groups that live a distance apart cannot understand one another. Because of this, Dagbane, the language spoken in the Dagomba region, has become a lingua franca, a language which people must learn to be able to do business with other groups. However, when northern speakers and southern speakers meet they almost always communicate in English, which has become another lingua franca. Thus northern Ghanaians usually know their own language and the language of their nearest neighbors, Dagbane as the northern lingua franca, and English as the national lingua franca.

Thanks to the efforts of the missionaries, Twi, Ashanti, Fanti, Ewe, Ga, Dagbane, and many local languages have written forms today.

WRITING SYSTEMS

All Ghanaian languages existed only in a spoken form until the missionaries arrived in West Africa. In order to bring the message of the Bible to the local people, missionaries set out to learn the local languages and create a written script for them. Because many of the missionaries who learned and transcribed the languages were linguists, they often wrote the dialects in the orthography of linguistics. Thus all over Ghana today signs and notices written in local languages have some characters that are not in the Roman alphabet.

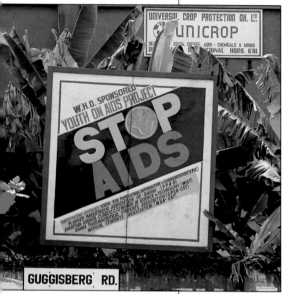

A billboard campaign against the spread of AIDS.

ENGLISH

A native speaker of English who arrives in Ghana and stands on the street listening may have considerable difficulty recognizing the language being spoken. Not only is the accent different, the way words are put together is also different. Many of the African languages are tonal. This means that the tone of the voice alters the meaning of the word, just as in Chinese. Some Ghanaians have transferred this tonal system to English.

Another difficulty English speakers might encounter is unfamiliar vocabulary. In the United States and Britain some of the vocabulary has changed over the years, moving the two forms of English apart. So too in Ghana, where some old English words are still used together with new words from local languages or invented words. Other familiar English words have taken on new meanings.

For example, the word "dash" has joined the Ghanaian form of English and means "give." Originally a Portuguese word, it has replaced "give" in local English.

The word "sister" is used more widely than in British English. In Ghana it can be used as a friendly form of address to any young woman, for example, schoolfriends would call each other sister. Another expression is "my dear." In American English, it is a way of being friendly to someone. In Ghanaian English, it means girlfriend or boyfriend. Someone might therefore say, "I saw your my dear at church this morning," meaning "I saw your boyfriend." In British English, calling someone an "old crow" is a term of abuse, but in Ghanaian English it is a compliment, meaning that the person is wise and clever.

In some cases this form of English has become almost a new language, known as pidgin English, with not only its own vocabulary, but a different grammar system based on local languages. Often the verbs "is" or "have" are left out and the letter "s" is left off the ends of words. In other cases the word is repeated to make a plural. In many regions teachers find it easier to teach their pupils in the local pidgin version of English for the first few years and then move on to standard English in the senior years. Since many children do not go beyond elementary school, pidgin English is the only form they learn. Generally the longer a student has been in school the closer his or her English becomes to that understood and used in the United States or Britain.

*Ghana has three national newspapers—*Daily Graphic, The Ghanaian Times *and* The Pioneer. *There is considerable freedom of the press today, although in the past this was not the case. Two of the newspapers are government-owned and cover national news rather than international news.*

LINGUISTS

Among many of the tribes of Ghana an important member of the chief's entourage is the *okyeame* ("otch-ee-AH-mee") or linguist. He accompanies the chief on all his official duties and carries a special symbol of office, a mace. His job is to listen to what the chief says and translate it for the people, even if the chief and his people speak the same language. His real job is as a language master of sorts. He spends his apprenticeship learning how to say things in the most euphemistic and flattering way.

For every thing that the chief wants to say there is a polite and diplomatic way of saying it. The chief merely concentrates on the substance of his message, while the linguist retells it for him in a literary and decorative way. The linguist may not add any new information to the chief's words, but he can refer back to ancient stories or create a beautiful image. He polishes the chief's words for him. Among some tribes the linguist also mediates between the chief and his subjects. The chief whispers to the linguist what he wants to say and the linguist makes the chief's words fit into a set of well-known proverbs.

A grandmother tells the village children a folk tale.

PROVERBS AND STORIES

Much of Ghanaian folk wisdom is contained in a vast set of proverbs that are well-known to everyone in the country. These proverbs are told to children as a set of moral tales that teach them the values of the family. They are often written or drawn on everyday objects. Mammy wagons, for example, always have some message or drawing painted on the front. Sometimes these aphorisms, such as "The Lord is my shepherd" or "God is good," are taken from Christian or Muslim texts. More cryptic messages, written in English or a local language, might be "poor no friend," meaning poverty is no friend to people. Both the truck driver and his truck are known by its caption.

Moral tales include stories about the naughty spider Ananse. He is part human and part spider and is very wicked. He tries to cheat people, but always turns out to be too clever for his own good. The stories about him are fun and teach children to be good.

NAMES

In southern Ghana people are named after the day on which they were born. This means that there are only 14 possible names: seven men's names—Kwajo (Monday), Kwabena, Kwaku, Yaw, Kofi, Kwame, and Kwesi—and seven women's names—Adjoa, Abena, Akua, Yaa, Efua, Ama, and Esi. Thus Kofi Annan was born on a Friday, while Kwame Nkrumah was born on a Saturday. In addition each child is given a name chosen by its father, usually the name of a particularly respected ancestor. When two children in the same family are born on the same day they will be given a number too, so two brothers both born on Friday will be called Kofi and Kofi Manu ("second Kofi").

Other ways of naming a child might be to give a name that recalls some feature of their birth. An unexpected child born on Friday would be named Kofi Nyamekye ("God given"). A child born after the loss of a previous baby might be called Ababio ("the returned one"), meaning that the dead child has returned in the body of the new baby. In addition to the two names there might be others, depending on the parents' wishes. Many people in the cities also take Christian names so that people have a minimum of three names and a maximum of ten or more. Children do not take the names of their parents at all, so within a family everyone's names are completely different unless they were born on the same day!

In the days before telephones the drummers of talking drums learned to beat out messages like a kind of Morse code, but the sounds that the drum made actually copied the sound of the words they conveyed. Today these drums are used for ceremonial purposes, where once they carried important messages over hundreds of miles.

TALKING DRUMS

Like many other countries in West Africa, Ghana has a tradition of talking drums. These are drums that are used as a means of communication rather than to make music. They are hourglass-shaped, with skins stretched over both ends and joined by tightly drawn rawhide cords. As the cords are stretched or released by the drummer the tone of the drum changes, following the tonal pattern of the language that it is copying.

ARTS

AS IN MANY OTHER AFRICAN CULTURES, the distinction between leisure, art, religion, and festivals in Ghana is a vague one. Ghanaian traditional arts and crafts evolved as a part of the religious and domestic needs of the people, while dance and music were, and still are, forms of worship and expressions of kinship. These early art forms have since evolved into a more modern music, art, and literature in Ghana today.

MUSIC

Music is an integral part of Ghanaian life and culture. When a folk story is performed it is usually accompanied by music, using either traditional instruments or more modern sounds. Music and singing accompany a Ghanaian's life, from daily work to major life events, such as birth, puberty, and funerals.

Opposite: **A potter at work in Accra.**

Left: **A poster artist in Kumasi. Ghana's modern artists work with oil and watercolors and regularly exhibit their work in international exhibitions. Ato Delaquis, Victor Butler, and Victor Odoi use conventional materials, but adapt them to traditional subjects of African life.**

Attendants blow tusk horns at an Ashanti festival.

Traditional music is played on four types of instruments—idiophones, such as rattles and xylophones, that vibrate naturally; membranophones, such as drums; aerophones, such as horns and pipes; and chordophones, or the many types of string instruments. The many instruments in Ghana have different uses within the various tribes.

Among some tribes their use is strictly restricted to certain religious events or may only be played for certain chiefs. The *nkofe* ("n-KOFF-eh") horns may only be used by the chief of the tribe, while the *kikaa* ("KEE-kah") horn is used only in the Dagomba region and for praise songs about the divisional chiefs. Another example is the *apirede* ("ap-eer-EH-deh") orchestra, made up of several drums, a gong, and clappers, which can only be played by the men whose job it is to carry the royal stools of the chiefs.

Some drums are thought to imitate the cries of certain animals. One makes the noise of a leopard, while another mimics a crocodile. They are played by tribes that have these animals as a totem.

Other drums are known as talking drums. One, the *atumpan* ("at-UM-pan") drum of the Akan people, mimics the tonal language of the people. It is a sacred drum and can only be made by certain people. The drummer himself must never make his own drum. The drum is made from a certain tree and the membrane is made from the ear of an elephant. The pegs that hold the membrane down are also made from a special tree. The varying tones of the drum are created by stretching or relaxing the pegs that hold down the membrane. The drum is played with a hammer often made from an elephant's tusk. This type of drum was once used to send messages from village to village, but its use is more ceremonial and cultural today.

Drummers at a festival. In a drum ensemble various drums are used in counterpoint to create varying rhythms.

Osibisa—a Ghanaian band that has found international fame with songs such as "Sunshine Day."

PALM WINE AND HIGHLIFE

The modern music of the Ashanti people is called palm wine. It is solo guitar music that originated in the small bars and drinking spots of southern Ghana. The singer plays an acoustic guitar and improvises songs on the spot about the customers or about politics. The songs are often uncomplimentary and can be hilarious.

Highlife originated in the port towns of southern Ghana in the 1920s and is a fusion of traditional drumming and European-style tunes. This kind of music gained international popularity in the 1950s after Ghanaian musicians such as E.T. Mensah discovered American jazz during World War II. Mensah formed a professional dance band like the big bands of 1940s America, but his style was uniquely African with powerful rhythms. By the 1950s there were many such bands in Ghana.

Another important figure of the time was King Bruce, who played saxophone and trumpet and led the Black Beats, a band of more than 20 musicians. He wrote songs in English and Ga. His career continued into the 1990s and his songs were put onto CDs in 1997. Many more bands and individuals have found fame in Europe and the United States, notably Osibisa, Highlife International, Kantata, and Pat Thomas. The most popular highlife musician in the 1990s is Alex Konadu.

DANCE

Like much else in Ghanaian art, dance plays a large part in the lives of ordinary people. It is an ancient tradition and each movement of the dancer often carries a symbolic as well as social meaning. The dances of

94

the various tribes are different in style and purpose. Particular movements are typical of the different tribes. The Akan tribes, for example, use complex footwork, combined with intricate hand and body movements. The dances of the Frafra are much simpler and are performed by columns of dancers moving in synchronization and concentrating on stamping movements, with few hand or body movements except swaying.

The Dagaba often incorporate stooping and leaping movements into their dances, while in northern Ghana the dances are more acrobatic, with tumbling and lifting. The dances of men and women also vary, with women's dancing being more sinuous and men's more angular and sharp. Individual movements carry symbolic meaning for the spectators. Reaching up to the sky indicates a call to God, while rolling the wrists together and drawing them sharply apart indicates the breaking of chains, or the freedom of the dancer. Mime often comes into play in the dances. Funeral dances are often solemn and slow, while birth, puberty, and wedding dances are faster and more exciting.

ARTS AND CRAFTS

The most famous artifacts of Ghana are *kente* cloth and the gold weights and stools of the Ashanti chiefs. Among many tribes the cloth is a printed cotton, but among the Ashanti tribes the cloth is woven in strips with intricate designs and is very valuable. Traditionally it was woven only by men, although a few women have now learned the skill. In the 19th century weavers began buying silk from European traders and weaving it into the design. The woven motifs are geometric and each person has his own style. The Ashanti chiefs have their own royal weavers, who make cloth for the chiefs and their mothers.

Each color and geometric design has its own meaning. Gold and yellow indicate God, royalty, eternal life, and prosperity. White represents purity and joy, while green is newness and fertility. Red stands for death, and plain red outfits are worn at funerals. Blue represents both love and the power of the queen mothers. Circles show the presence of God, triangles fertility and womanhood, and rectangles virility and manhood.

Ancestral stools are another art form whose significance is far more than artistic in Ghanaian society. Each boy or girl has a stool made when they are children, and the stool comes to represent their life energy. Each person keeps their own stool all their life and when they die their body is seated on the stool while it is prepared for burial. After death the stool goes to the ancestral huts and is revered by the family as the spirit of the dead person.

The stools are made of three pieces—a rectangular base, a seat that is curved, and a carved supporting pillar or pillars, where the importance and character of the owner is described. For a wealthy chief or a rich man the stool is intricately carved. In all cases the symbolism of the carvings is important. Some stools are plated with silver or, in the case of the early Ashanti kings, with gold. After death each person's stool is treated with egg yolk, soot, and sheep's blood, symbolizing peace and caution. Stool carvers are craftsmen and religious figures. When the wood for a stool is cut, religious rituals are performed.

Another art form that is also part of tribal religious beliefs is the carving of wooden figures. These may be kept in totem or fetish houses, where they represent the animist gods, or they may become intermediaries between the people and the animist gods. An infertile woman may carry a carved wooden doll on her back that would take her wish for children and may bring help from the animist spirits. Other such dolls may be placed around houses or on the outskirts of the village to protect the tribe. The dolls represent each tribe's vision of beauty and may be scarified or carved to represent the fertility of a woman or the angular qualities of men.

Above: **Many wooden carvings carry religious meanings.**

Opposite: **A man sews strips of *kente* cloth together.**

COFFINS AS ART

Funerals are lavish and expensive affairs in Ghana, and the more important the deceased the more elaborate their funeral. In recent years an unusual art form has developed around the funerals of some Ghanaians, where coffin makers are commissioned to make a coffin that matches the occupation of the deceased.

Thus a fisherman's coffin might be a huge tuna fish carved out of wood and painted, while a truck driver's coffin might be a small replica of the truck he drove. A pineapple farmer might be buried in a pineapple-shaped coffin, while a rich man might be buried in a model of a Cadillac. People often commission their coffins long before they die since the work on each coffin is elaborate and may take months of work. If the person dies before his coffin is completed the funeral is delayed until it is ready. Not surprisingly, these coffins are very expensive.

ARCHITECTURE

Ghana has an interesting architectural mix of centuries-old castles and forts built by the Portuguese and British, modern buildings erected since the 1960s, and the indigenous building styles of the various tribes.

Nothing remains of the city built by the Ashanti at Kumasi except some engravings. The engravings show complex structures built around central courtyards. Walls, doors, and shutters were intricately carved and in the case of palaces, were covered in silver or gold leaf. A royal pavilion has been constructed at the cultural center in Kumasi, showing what such a building would have been like.

The facade of Nkrumah Museum in Accra.

THE LOST WAX PROCESS

This process was used by the Ashanti when they made the gold weights that became part of the Ashanti chief's symbols of office. The process was first noticed among the people of Benin. They used it to make large but intricate bronze statues, but the Ashanti use the technique with gold. First a model of the weight is produced by building up a core made of loamy soil and water. After thorough drying this core is covered in a layer of bees' wax. The wax is carved and decorated with a bone tool. When the carving is complete the whole object is covered in more layers of soil and sticks are pushed through all three layers to hold the mold together. The mold is dried again with the wax completely sealed inside. A pit is dug and the mold is fired until the wax melts. Then the empty space created by the melted wax is filled with molten gold. After the gold has cooled the earth is dug away from the outside and the core of the gold figure.

Colonial architecture in Kumasi.

Modern rural buildings are far more humble. In the south they are square buildings, often built around a central courtyard and with a corrugated iron roof. At the entrance to the compound is a loggia, where guests are greeted. The walls are made of dried mud and are constantly reconstructed and decorated by the women who live in the house.

In the villages of the north a series of circular huts are built around a central courtyard. Roofs are pointed and thatched. In the far north roofs are terraced and form a flat space for drying crops or for the family to sleep during hot weather. The walls are clay or unfired earth and are decorated either with paint or designs etched into the drying mud. Inside, the buildings are often simple, with a kitchen area opening onto the courtyard and several sleeping rooms.

In the cities, domestic architecture is Western in style. The bungalows of richer people have yards and a parking space for the car. Public housing consists of apartment blocks in various states of modernity.

SYMBOLS

Symbolism is an important part of the lives of Ghanaians. It can be seen in the design of *kente* cloth, in the patterns on the walls of huts, and in many other art forms. The chief's garments and jewelry are not just adornments. Each piece tells a story of the chief's origins, his wealth, and the history of the tribe. These symbols can be seen in other aspects of Ghanaian life, such as on canoes, mammy wagons, ornamental gourds, stools, and cooking utensils.

A chameleon symbolizes a mixture of slowness and quickness as well as the unreliability of words, which can change just like the chameleon's colors. A snail and a tortoise together symbolize the desire for peace, since neither of these creatures is ever hunted or shot at. A human figure holding its ear and pointing to its eye indicates that blindness does not prevent understanding in other ways. All of these symbols carved onto domestic items remind the owners of popular Ghanaian proverbs.

LITERATURE

The earliest form of literature in Ghana were the stories told over and over again by professional storytellers, who added to and updated the stories each time they were told. The stories would be told at special events, such as weddings or funerals, and accompanied by music and singing. Storytelling often formed the means by which the values of the extended family or tribe were passed on to the next generation. As tribal life gives way to modern city life, there is a fear that these stories will be lost. However, some of this tradition is being revitalized today by people such as Koo Nimo (Daniel Amponsah), who broadcasts modern versions of the ancient stories on Ghanaian radio. He maintains the moral and cultural aspects of the stories he tells, but like his predecessors he updates the stories to bring in modern politics and issues. The stories are told at traditional ceremonies and are accompanied by guitar and percussion.

Today many Ghanaian writers have gained recognition as novelists, poets, and playwrights. Some successful Ghanaian writers include Christina Ama Ata Aidoo, K.A. Bediako, George Awoonor-Williams, and Ayi Kwei Armah, who wrote the powerful novel *The Beautiful Ones Are Not Yet Born*, about life in a newly independent African country. Christina Ama Ata Aidoo is one of a small number of female African writers and has written *The Dilemma of a Ghost* and *Anowa*.

A dilemma facing African writers is whether to write in their mother tongue or to write in the language of colonial times. The latter would bring their work to a larger world audience, but carries with it echoes of the colonial past. On the other hand writing in the mother tongue restricts most Ghanaian writers to an audience of no more than half their country's population.

LEISURE

GHANAIANS LOVE MUSIC, DANCING, and good company. In the villages all these ingredients come together in the many festivals and community events that fill the calendar, especially in the period following the yam harvest. In the cities the tribal and family structures have given way to a more urban lifestyle, and nuclear families find their leisure in the churches, markets, restaurants, bars, and clubs common in the larger towns and cities. Ghanaians are essentially gregarious and outgoing people who welcome strangers to their homes and love giving and receiving gifts.

LEISURE IN THE CITIES

Most of the larger cities are in the south of Ghana, where the tourism industry is also based. Accra has a flourishing nightlife, with many bars

Opposite: **Ghanaians enjoy a day at the beach.**

Left: **Boys race with homemade wheels.**

A band entertains music club patrons.

and music clubs that offer live music. A typical form of entertainment in the city is a concert party, which includes a play, a stand-up comic act, and music, while the audience drinks *akpeteshe* ("ak-pet-ESH-ee," distilled palm wine). Ghana is the home of highlife music, an African big band sound that uses Western instruments to produce African rhythms. In the large cities this style of music is enjoyed at concert parties and in the churches, where a form of gospel highlife has developed.

Accra has nearly 40 churches in its city center alone. These form the focus of social life for many people, and on Sundays music and singing can be heard in many of the churches, especially the indigenous African ones. Favorite meeting places include the foodstalls and "chop houses" inexpensive café-style places, found all over the cities. European and Asian restaurants can also be found in the city centers. The movie theater is popular, with African and Western movies vying for popularity with kung fu movies. Ghana has a National Theater, where locals and tourists can enjoy cultural shows and modern theater.

LEISURE IN THE COUNTRY

In rural areas leisure often takes second place to the grueling demands of the farming year. Leisure is more closely related to the festivals and traditions of the African religions than to the spare time or available cash of the people who live in the villages. As many rural people live at a subsistence level leisure is found in activities that also benefit the family group. If they have spare time after the harvest or while the crops are growing men will go out and hunt small animals.

In the countryside many villages do not yet have a permanent supply of electricity, so events such as concert parties and movies are not common. However, there are many traveling movie theaters that tour the villages, carrying their own generator and showing videos or movies. If there are no clubs, bars, or spare cash, young people gather in the village square at sunset and sing together or play games well into the night. Many villagers have battery-powered radios, but in most small towns there are loudspeaker systems broadcasting radio programs in the streets.

Men and women shake
hands, whether friends
or complete strangers.
When Ghanaians meet,
everyone shakes hands
with everyone else, with
no precedence to age or
sex.

VISITING

Ghanaians enjoy visiting one another's homes. Greetings are very important among Ghanaians and strangers will greet one another in the street. Usually the person in movement begins the greeting, so when people visit a home it is their job to begin. The host welcomes his guests with the word *akwaba* ("ak-WAH-bah"). The guests bring a gift of food or even money that will be left discreetly with the woman of the house. The guests are greeted at the entrance or loggia of the house and are then brought inside and sat down. A glass of water is offered and it is impolite to refuse. Then the host asks the guests why they have come.

This is a tradition known as *amanee* ("ah-MAH-nee"). The family listens while the guests give an account of their journey and reason for coming. Then the host gives a brief account of the recent events in the family, after which he stands again and repeats his welcome. The handshakes are repeated. When this formal part of the visit is over, everyone chats away. *Akpeteshe* might be brought out.

SPORTS AND GAMES

The most popular sport in Ghana is soccer. Popular, too, are boxing, ping pong, hockey, basketball, cricket, and track and field. Ghanaians also play a game similar to cricket called *apaat* ("ap-AHT").

Children love to play games of make-believe, accompanied by songs. Girls usually play separately from boys, but sometimes the children's games bring them together. Traditional games include a game similar to checkers, marbles, and *oware* ("oh-WAR-eh"), a game similar to backgammon played on the ground with seeds or pebbles.

BUYING AND SELLING

Soccer games in Ghana often draw large and enthusiastic crowds of spectators.

Buying and selling in the village market is a long, drawn-out but enjoyable process involving much chatting and much bargaining. The buyer mentions an item she wishes to buy and the vendor points out the high quality of the item, cost of production, difficulties in transportation, and so on, and names a price. The buyer pretends to be shocked at the price and so the negotiations begin. When the sale is completed the buyer may ask for extras. If vegetables were bought, the "extras" might be salt or cooking spices, or a couple of smaller vegetables to go with it. The more produce that has been bought, the more the buyer can expect as extras.

In the city the same process of bargaining takes place over goods in the markets, although the extras are usually only included with foodstuffs. In department stores prices are fixed. Just as in the rest of the world, shopping in department stores or even in markets is often a leisure activity.

FESTIVALS

OVER A HUNDRED FESTIVALS ARE CELEBRATED IN GHANA. Most of these predate Christianity or Islam and have their origins in the animist religions that are indigenous to Ghana. They largely follow the cycle of the seasons, with harvest festivals being the major festivals celebrated throughout the country. Most regions have yam festivals that mark the first yam harvests or the end of the harvesting season.

Other festivals celebrate the arrival of the tribe into Ghana or pay remembrance to the ancestors. Some mark a new start in the year and involve cleaning out the house or clearing the land around the village. Originally religious in nature, they reaffirmed the tribe's belief in the spirit world. Today, however, they are more cultural. Celebrations center around the tribe's chief—the custodian of the tribe's traditions. He has advisers who help him to determine the correct date for a festival and the way it should be celebrated.

Opposite and left: **Tribal festivals remain an important part of Ghanaian life today.**

DURBARS

The highlight of every festival, the *durbar* ("DERR-bar"), is a kind of pageant. In it the chief of the tribe is dressed in his finest clothes and seated on a palanquin, a chair carried by several of his servants. He is shielded from the heat of the sun by a large, colorful umbrella. The lower chieftains follow in the procession, also adorned in their finest clothes. The chiefs are carried to the place where the festival is to take place and their attendants—the executioners of older times—tell stories of past triumphs in battle. Each lesser chief goes before the regional chief to offer his allegiance, taking off his crown and one shoe and bowing before him. The chief then makes a speech to his people and the festival begins.

In the past people were allowed time off from work to return to their tribal lands to celebrate important festivals. Anyone who did not take part in the ceremonies could be fined, though this rule has been relaxed as many people now live in the cities and contact with the home village has become less frequent. Families would go to the edge of town to wait for their relatives and escort them home with much music and singing. The festivals have thus become a time for returning home, settling old feuds and land disputes, and for having a good time. All festivals, even the sad ones, involve a great deal of dancing, singing, feasting, and drinking.

Dancing girls in colorful dresses go through the steps they have learned for a festival.

ODWIRA

This is the festival at which the new harvest of yams is presented to the ancestors. This festival is practiced all over Ghana, particularly among the Akan people. The celebration itself lasts about a week, but preparations last 40 days, through an entire *adae*. It usually takes place in September or October, depending on the harvest. All consumption of new yams is prohibited until the festival is over. Forty days before the festival all singing, dancing, and noise in the village is banned. Even funerals, which are usually noisy affairs, must be quiet. Seven days before the festival the path to the mausoleum of the past chiefs is swept. Six days before, tubers of the new yam harvest are paraded through the streets. A procession goes to the mausoleum with a sheep and rum to awaken the spirit of the Odwira. The procession returns to the chief and a blessing and purification ritual takes place. Drummers play through the night.

On the fifth day before the festival the village is silent and the people fast and remember their dead ancestors. Everyone wears brown clothes and red turbans to commemorate the dead. On the fourth day before, a huge feast is held for both the living and the dead. Unsalted cooked yam and chicken are taken in procession and laid at a shrine on the outskirts of town. The food for the dead chiefs is at the head of the procession, shaded by huge, colorful umbrellas. In every home food is laid out for anyone to eat and there is a main feast in the center of town. That night there is another ceremony, this time accompanied by drumming and singing. Everyone stays inside

An Ashanti chief in his finery at a festival in Kumasi.

111

A procession of chiefs' stools in Elmina.

their homes as the dead chiefs' stools are paraded through the town to the stream for their annual ceremonial cleansing. Only privileged people are allowed to see these stools. The final day of the festival is the great *durbar*, where all the neighboring chiefs arrive to show their respect and pledge allegiance to the regional chief. They parade through the streets of the town, carried on palanquins and accompanied by drummers and servants carrying gold swords and guns. Then the chiefs settle in the central square and performances of dancing and singing take place. Drinks and food are offered and the local chiefs reaffirm their loyalty to the regional chief.

The various tribes of the Akan all celebrate different versions of this festival, but the essential elements are the same—the dead are remembered and thanked for the new yam harvest, the chiefs take part in the *durbar*, and a great feast is held.

SOME OTHER FESTIVALS

THE AYERYE This is a Fanti festival in which the young men of the tribe are initiated into the clan of their father. Each young man is only a member of his mother's clan until puberty, when he is officially taken into his father's militia. The festival takes place between September and December, usually to coincide with the harvest festival.

THE DEER HUNT FESTIVAL In Winneba a 300-year-old festival is held in which two competing teams hunt deer. The winning team is the first one to bring back the game. The trick is that the deer must be caught with only sticks and cudgels. The festival usually takes place in May.

Participants at a Fanti festival near Accra.

THE SAMANPID FESTIVAL Among the Kusasi people in the Sapeliga region of northern Ghana this is a thanksgiving festival carried out at the end of the harvest. The festival takes place in the house of every extended family.

THE PATH CLEARING FESTIVAL This festival dates back to the time before modern roads, when it was the duty of each citizen of the village to return home once a year and help clear the village paths, particularly those to the shrines and the village well. It is an Akan festival, practiced among the Gomua and Agona tribes.

Nowadays there may be no path clearing at all, but the festival is still a good reason for families to return home and have some fun. The festival usually takes place just before the new yams are introduced to the ancestors.

FOOD

IN SOME AREAS OF GHANA, especially in the north where weather conditions can be extreme, hunger can pose a serious problem for almost half the year. In the north food is harvested during a long, dry season that follows a wet season that is sometimes too short for the growing crops. This is followed by another period when new crops are sown and when much energy is needed to look after the fields.

In the south the climate is less harsh. There are cities where food can be stored more efficiently and most people have money and can buy some of their food. In the east there is very fertile soil, abundant rainfall, and a mild climate, and large farms produce both cash crops and staples that are transported to the cities.

Opposite: **Cola nuts for sale.**

Left: **The Kumasi market is a hive of activity, with many different types of vegetables and fruit bought and sold each day.**

STAPLES

These are the foods that make up the bulk of a person's diet. In the West this is often wheat, potatoes, or to a lesser extent, rice. In Ghana the staple foods vary according to the region. In the north millet, yams, and corn are the staple foods, while in the south and west, plantains, cassava, and cocoyams are grown. Across to the southeast, which is drier, corn and cassava are the staple foods.

In the center of the country there are also areas where rice is grown and makes up part of the diet. Both hill rice and wet rice are grown and eaten in Ghana. Rice is useful because it is easy to store.

Cocoyam grows in the forest regions of Ghana. It is the root of a low-growing plant and needs warm, damp soil. Some cocoyam plants are harvested for the shoots, while others are collected for the roots. An indigenous plant, it grows wild throughout the forested region, but it is also cultivated.

Cassava is a root vegetable that grows in a wide range of conditions, with some species tolerating the dry climate of the north, and others preferring the wet forest belt. It is turned by a complex process into flour. In its raw state it contains a form of cyanide and, if not processed properly, is poisonous. The tubers can be left in the soil until they are needed, and cassava is often the last food staple left at the end of the dry season. Corn and millet are grains that grow in full sun and can tolerate fairly dry conditions. Both the grain and flour are cooked.

A fish market in Accra. In Ghana fish is more commonly eaten than meat.

MEAT AND FISH

Meat is a rare luxury in many Ghanaians' diet. In the rural areas animals represent wealth and so are rarely slaughtered. They provide a form of currency and are often used as dowry payments or are bartered at the market for imported goods. When they do appear in meals it is usually as an ingredient in a stew rather than as the main course. Fish is more common and again appears as a part of a stew.

OTHER FOODS

Groundnuts are an important source of protein and grow mostly in the north. Palm nuts form the basis of most soups and stews. Green vegetables include the leaves of the cocoyam, known as *kontomire* ("kon-toh-MEER-eh"), a form of spinach, okra, as well as eggplants, onions, tomatoes, sweet potatoes, and many kinds of beans. There are also several vegetables that only grow in particular areas of Ghana and are unknown in other parts.

A family peels plantain to prepare *fufu*, a popular Ghanaian dish. Plantain is a type of banana, but is much bigger. It needs a high temperature, high humidity, and high rainfall to grow well. Its fruit is starchier than the banana and is most nutritious just before it ripens, so it is picked while still green. It can be made into meal, refined into flour, or boiled or fried while still fresh.

THE DAILY MEALS

Usually three meals are eaten a day. In the countryside where there is much work to be done, the midday meal might be only a snack and the breakfast a more substantial meal. In the home the family separates at mealtimes. The men eat their food from one bowl, taking turns to help themselves with their right hand. The women and girls share another bowl of food, while the boys eat together. There are rules about who eats the meat or fish first and how it is to be shared.

The most commonly eaten evening meal in Ghana is *fufu*, a dough made from a mixture of cassava and either plantain or cocoyam. It is served with a soup that might be made from groundnuts, palm fruit, fish, beans, or other vegetables, or a mixture of several items, all simmered for an hour. The soups that include groundnuts are usually thick and grainy, while those made with palm fruit have a thick, yellow, oily base. Other stews have special names—*forowe* ("foh-ROH-weh") is a fish stew with tomatoes, while *nkita* ("n-KEE-tah") is a stew of eggs, fish, and beef.

Chilies are commonly grown and used in Ghanaian cooking and a favorite soup is pepper soup, which is hot and peppery.

A popular breakfast dish called *ampesi* ("am-PEH-si") consists of cassava, cocoyam, yam, and plantain mixed together, boiled, and pounded and then boiled again with onion and fish.

Another common base for a meal is *kenkey* ("ken-KAY"), which is made from corn meal. The meal is ground and soaked in water and left to ferment for two days. Then the result is formed into balls and dropped into boiling water. After an hour the mash is wrapped in plantain leaf packages and will keep for two days. It is eaten with fish or stew as a substitute for *fufu*. Similar fermented dough is made from corn meal or millet in the north of the country. The Ewe make a version from corn dough and cassava mash.

Food stalls such as this offer Ghanaians inexpensive meals.

SWEET DISHES

There are many sweet dishes in Ghana. Surprisingly though, not many of them are made from chocolate, despite the fact that chocolate is cheap and of very good quality in Ghana. Some sweet dishes are built around the staple starchy vegetables. One popular dish is *tartare* ("TAR-tar"), or pancakes made from ripe plantain, pounded and deep-fried in palm oil. Mixed with cornflour and made into balls like doughnuts, the plantain becomes *krako* ("KRAH-koe"). With boiled soybeans added, it is *aboboe* ("ah-BO-bo-ee"). Sweet dishes are not served after the main course, but are eaten as snacks at any time of the day.

A snack vendor fries bean cakes.

EATING OUT

As Ghana has a growing tourist industry there are many restaurants that cater both to foreigners and to the wealthier Ghanaians, especially in the towns along the southern coast. Foreign cuisine is common, especially European-style, Indian, and Chinese. Less expensive are the "chop houses," which are café-style places selling local food. The cheapest way of eating out is at a street stall, usually run by a woman, selling rice with various dishes. A popular street snack is *kelewele* ("ke-leh-WEH-leh"), or fried plantains seasoned with ginger and chili. *Koko* ("KO-ko") is corn or millet porridge mixed with milk and sugar. Other stalls sell slices of fresh fruit or coconuts that are slashed open on the spot for the customer to enjoy the water and meat.

DRINKS

As readily available in Ghana as in the rest of the world are the ubiquitous cola drinks. Ghana produces some soft drinks of its own, such as Refresh, a fizzy drink made with fresh fruit juice, and Supermalt, a dark-colored drink tasting of malt. Beer is popular. Ghana was the first West African country to have a brewery. There are several local beers nowadays as well as imported beers. More unusual drinks include ice *kenkey*, which is the northern fermented corn flour dissolved in water and fermented further. Another unusual taste more common in the north is *pito* ("PEE-toh") beer, made from millet rather than hops. In the south the drink of choice is palm wine, which can range from very alcoholic or almost non-alcoholic.

THE KITCHEN

The traditional kitchen in rural houses contains a wood-burning open hearth that is recoated every day in fresh white clay. Standing in the hearth is a tripod for holding the stew pot, while fresh wood is stacked up at the side, ready for use. There is also a covered oven, fueled by charcoal, which is used for faster cooking, such as frying. Assorted pots and pans are kept in a chest. These often include a big cauldron for cooking stews and a large iron griddle for frying. Out in the yard would be two mortars and pestles—a tall one for crushing small nuts and grains and a larger one for pounding cassava and plantains to make the *fufu* or *kenkey*.

GARI BISCUITS

5 cassavas	6 oz (150 g) sugar
3 eggs	1 teaspoon nutmeg
milk	1 tablespoon flour

Peel, clean, and grate the cassavas. Beat the eggs and milk together. Add the grated cassava. Add the sugar and nutmeg. Sieve in the flour and mix well. Roll out and cut into cookie shapes. Bake in a hot oven for 15 minutes.

Women in northern Ghana prepare *pito* beer.

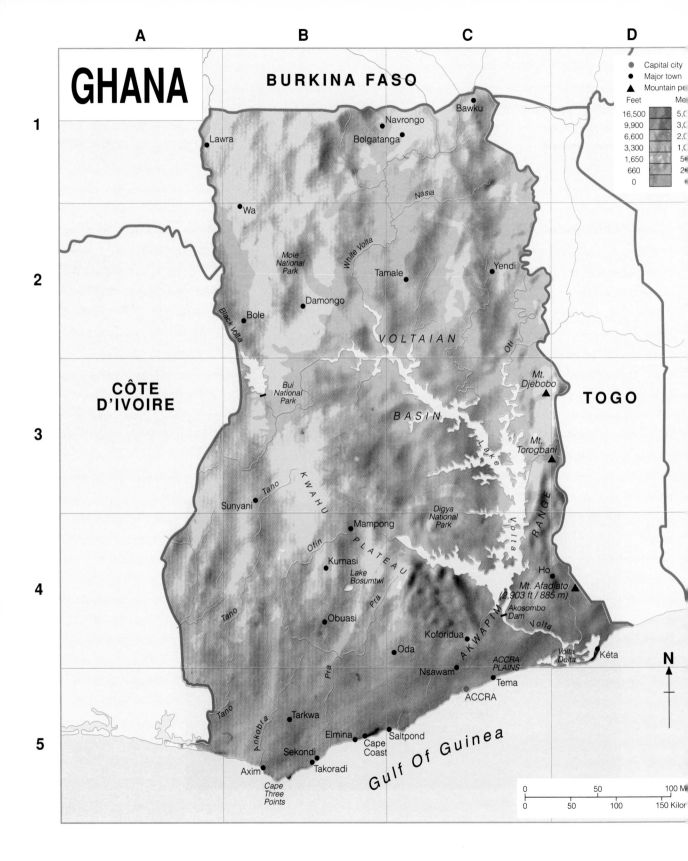

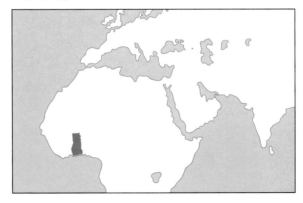

QUICK NOTES

AREA
92,100 square miles
(238,539 square km)

POPULATION
16.5 million (1995 estimate)

CAPITAL
Accra

OFFICIAL NAME
The Republic of Ghana

OFFICIAL LANGUAGE
English

HIGHEST POINT
Afadjato (2,903 ft / 885 m)

MAJOR LAKE
Lake Volta

MAIN ETHNIC GROUPS
Akan, Dagomba, Ewe, Ga-Adangme, Guan

MAIN RELIGIONS
Christianity, traditional African beliefs, Islam

RIVERS
Volta, Black Volta, White Volta, Oti

CLIMATE
Tropical, with temperatures generally between
70°F (21°C) and 90°F (32°C)

MAJOR CITIES
Kumasi, Tamale, Tema, Sekondi-Takoradi

NATIONAL FLAG
Three equal horizontal stripes, of red, yellow,
and green, with a five-pointed black star in the
center of the yellow stripe.

CURRENCY
The cedi
1 cedi = 100 pesewas
US$1 = 2,216 cedi

MAIN EXPORTS
Cocoa and cocoa products, timber and timber
products, gold, electricity

MAJOR IMPORTS
Machinery and transport equipment, petroleum
and petroleum products, chemicals

POLITICAL LEADERS
Kwame Nkrumah—prime minister from 1957
to 1960, president from 1960 to 1966.
Jerry Rawlings—assumed power as chairman
of Provisional National Defense Council in
1981, president since 1992.

ANNIVERSARIES
Independence Day (March 6)
Republic Day (July 1)

GLOSSARY

abosom ("ah-BOH-som")
Akan name for an animist spirit.

abusa ("ah-BOO-sah")
Clan or family grouping.

adae ("AHD-ay")
A period of 40 days in the Akan calendar.

akpeteshe ("ak-pet-ESH-ee")
Distilled palm wine.

akwaba ("ak-WAH-bah")
Welcome.

amanee ("ah-MAH-nee")
Custom of asking and explaining reasons for a visit.

apaat ("ap-AHT")
A game similar to cricket.

apirede ("ap-eer-EH-deh")
A traditional orchestra consisting of drums, gongs, and clappers, played by Ashanti stool carriers.

atumpan ("at-UM-pan")
Talking drum of the Akan.

bogya ("BOG-yah")
Physical aspect of a human being.

durbar ("DERR-bar")
Pageant during a festival.

enstoolment
The ceremony of establishing a new chief.

fetish house
A building dedicated to an animist spirit.

fufu ("FOO-foo")
A staple food made from cassava and either plantain or cocoyam.

highlife
African big band music.

juju
A form of medicine practiced by animist priests.

kente ("KEN-tey")
Traditional Ashanti cloth.

nton ("n-TON")
The spiritual aspect of being.

okyeame ("otch-ee-AH-mee")
Linguist who accompanies the chief.

oware ("oh-WAR-eh")
Traditional game, a little like backgammon, played on the ground with seeds or pebbles.

pito ("PEE-toh")
A beer made from millet.

tro tro ("TRO tro")
A truck that functions as a taxi in towns.

BIBLIOGRAPHY

Africa. Victoria, Australia: Lonely Planet Publications, 1995.

Brace, Steve. *Ghana (Economically Developing Countries).* Hove, England: Wayland (Publishers) Ltd, 1994.

Edgerton, Robert B. *The Fall of the Asante Empire: The Hundred-Year War for Africa's Gold Coast.* New York: The Free Press, 1995.

Hadjor, Kofi Buenor. *Nkrumah and Ghana.* London: Kegan Paul International Limited, 1988.

Ray, Donald Iain. *Ghana: Politics, Economics, and Society (Marxist Regimes Series).* Boulder, Colorado: L. Rienner Publishers, 1986.

INDEX

INDEX

INDEX